MUFFINS
& QUICK BREADS

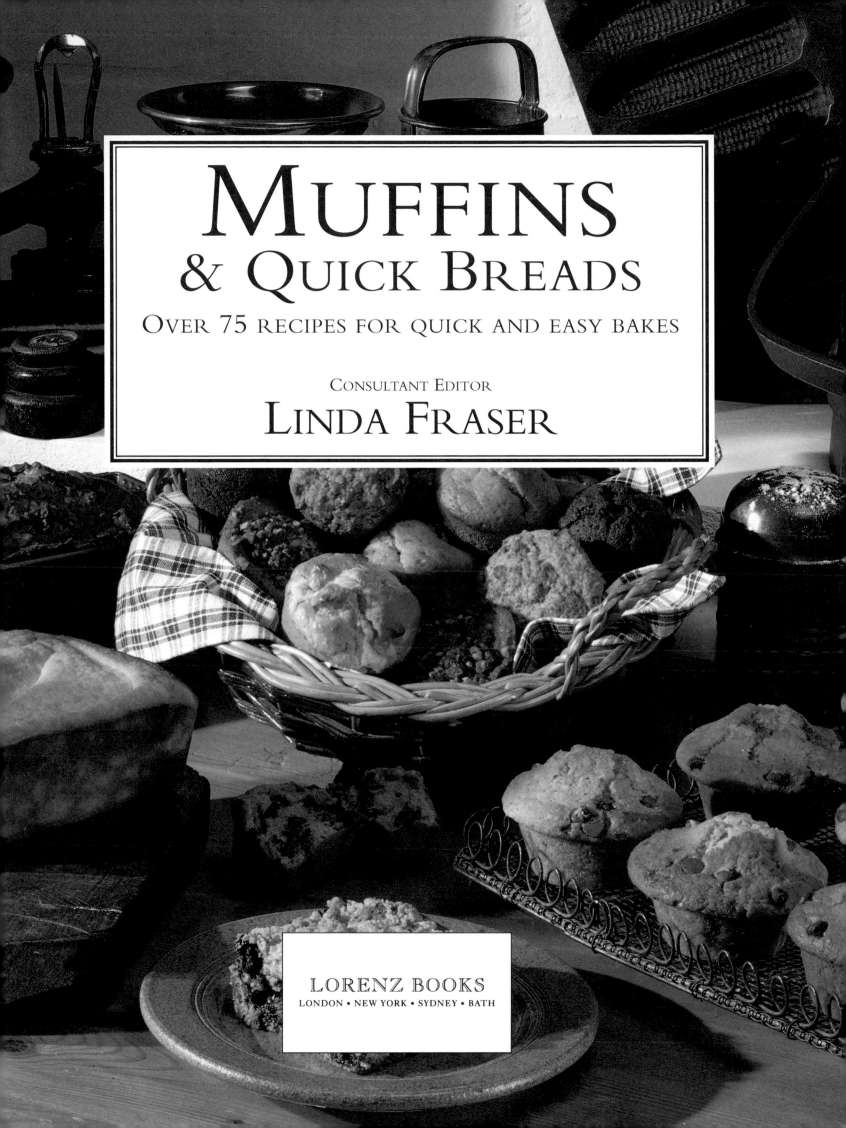

MUFFINS
& QUICK BREADS

OVER 75 RECIPES FOR QUICK AND EASY BAKES

CONSULTANT EDITOR

LINDA FRASER

LORENZ BOOKS
LONDON • NEW YORK • SYDNEY • BATH

First published by Lorenz Books in 1995

© 1995 Anness Publishing Limited

Lorenz Books is an imprint of
Anness Publishing Limited
Hermes House
88-89 Blackfriars Road
London SE1 8HA

This edition distributed in Canada by Book Express
an imprint of Raincoast Books Distribution Limited.

3 5 7 9 10 8 6 4 2

A CIP catalogue record for this book
is available from the British Library

Publisher: Joanna Lorenz
Senior Cookery Editor: Linda Fraser
Designer: Sheila Volpe
Jacket Designer: Siân Keogh
Photographers: Steve Baxter, Karl Adamson, Amanda Heywood,
James Duncan and Michelle Garrett
Food for Photography: Wendy Lee, Jane Stevenson and Elizabeth Wolf-Cohen
Props Stylists: Blake Minton and Kirsty Rawlings

Printed in Singapore by Star Standard Industries Pte. Ltd.

Recipes: Norma MacMillan, Carla Capalbo, Laura Washburn, Alex Barker, Sarah Gates, Shirley Gill,
Christine France, Hilaire Walden, Patricia Lousada, Katherine Richmond, Annie Nichols and Roz Denny

CONTENTS

BAKING TECHNIQUES

Baking your own muffins and breads is easy and satisfying, even if you're a beginner. Just follow the recipes and the tips, hints, and step-by-step techniques and you'll get perfect results every time.

1 ▲ For liquids measured in jugs: Use a glass or clear plastic measuring jug. Put the jug on a flat surface and pour in the liquid. Bend down and check that the liquid is exactly level with the marking on the jug, as specified in the recipe.

Equipment
To be able to cook efficiently and with pleasure, you need good equipment. That is not to say that you should invest in an extensive collection, but a basic range of cookware is essential. Buy the best equipment you can afford, adding more as your budget allows. Well made equipment lasts and is a sound investment; inexpensive cookware is likely to dent, break, or develop "hot spots" where food will stick and burn, so will need replacing. Flimsy tools make food preparation more time consuming.

2 ▲ For measuring dry ingredients in a spoon: Fill the spoon with the ingredient. Level the surface even with the rim of the spoon, using the straight edge of a knife.

3 ▲ For liquids measured in spoons: Pour the liquid into the measuring spoon, to the brim, and then pour it into the mixing bowl.

4 ▲ For measuring flour in a cup or spoon: Scoop the flour from the canister in the measuring cup or spoon. Hold it over the canister and level the surface.

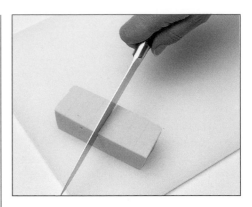

5 ▲ For measuring butter: Cut with a sharp knife and weigh, or cut off the specified amount following the markings on the wrapping paper.

6 ▲ For rectangular and square cake tins: Fold the paper and crease it with your fingernail to fit snugly into the corners of the tin. Then press the bottom paper lining into place.

7 ▲ To line muffin tins: Use paper cases of the required size. Or grease and flour the tins.

MAKING MUFFINS AND QUICK BREADS

As their name denotes, these bakes are fast and easy to make. The raising agent reacts quickly with moisture and heat to make the muffins and breads rise, without the need for a rising period before baking.

The raising agent is usually bicarbonate of soda or baking powder, which is a mixture of baking soda and an acid salt such as cream of tartar. It will start to work as soon as it comes into contact with liquid, so don't mix the dry and liquid ingredients until just before you are ready to fill the muffin tins and bake.

In addition to the thick-batter quick breads discussed here, there are also quick breads such as scones that are made from soft doughs.

Crunchy Muesli Muffins
Make the mixture from 5 oz (150 g) plain flour, 2½ teaspoons baking powder, 2 tablespoons caster sugar, 8 fl oz (250 ml) milk, 2 oz (50 g) melted butter or corn oil, and 1 egg, adding 7 oz (200 g) toasted oat cereal with raisins to the dry ingredients. Pour into muffin tins or deep bun tins. Bake in a 200°C/400°F/Gas 6 oven for 20 minutes or until golden brown. *Makes 10.*

1 ▲ For muffins: Combine the dry ingredients in a bowl. It is a good idea to sift the flour with the raising agent, salt and any spices to mix them evenly. Add the liquid ingredients and stir just until the dry ingredients are moistened; the mixture will not be smooth. Do not overmix attempting to remove all the lumps. If you do, the muffins will be tough and will have air holes in them.

2 ▲ Divide the mixture evenly among the greased muffin tins or deep bun tins lined with paper cases, filling them about two-thirds full. Bake until golden brown and a wooden skewer inserted in the centre comes out clean. To prevent soggy bottoms, remove the muffins immediately from the tins to a wire rack. Cool, and serve warm or at room temperature.

3 ▲ For fruit and/or nut teabreads: Method 1: Stir together all the liquid ingredients. Add the dry ingredients and beat just until smoothly blended. Method 2: Beat the butter with the sugar until the mixture is light and fluffy. Beat in the eggs followed by the other liquid ingredients. Stir in the dry ingredients. Pour the mixture into a prepared tin (typically a loaf tin). Bake until a wooden skewer inserted in the centre comes out clean. If the bread is browning too quickly, cover the top with foil.

4 ▲ Cool in the tin for 5 minutes, then turn out on to a wire rack to cool completely. A lengthways crack on the surface is characteristic of teabreads. For easier slicing, wrap the bread in greaseproof paper and overwrap in foil, then store overnight at room temperature.

MAKING FOCACCIA AND BREAD STICKS

Italian flatbreads, such as focaccia, and bread sticks can be topped with herbs and seeds for tasty accompaniments or starters. Personalize them with combinations of your favourite ingredients for unusual snacks, or split and fill flatbreads with ham or cheese for an Italian-style sandwich.

This basic dough can be used for other recipes, such as pizza. The dough may be frozen before it is baked, and thawed before filling.

1 ▲ For focaccia: Warm a mixing bowl by swirling some hot water in it. Drain. Place the yeast in the bowl, and pour on the warm water. Stir in the sugar, mix with a fork, and allow to stand until the yeast has dissolved and starts to foam, 5–10 minutes.

Working with yeast
Easy-blend (or fast-action) is the most readily available dried yeast. Unlike ordinary dried yeast, there is no need to mix it with liquid. Just combine it with the flour and other dry ingredients and then add the warm liquids.

If using fresh yeast, allow ½ oz (15 g) to each 1 tablespoon dried. Crumble it into a small bowl, add warm liquid and mash with a fork until blended.

If you are in any doubt about the freshness of ordinary dried or fresh yeast, set the mixture aside in a warm place; after 10 minutes or so it should be foamy.

2 ▲ Use a wooden spoon to mix in the salt and about one-third of the flour. Mix in another third of the flour, stirring with the spoon until the dough forms a mass and begins to pull away from the sides of the bowl.

3 ▲ Sprinkle some of the remaining flour onto a smooth work surface. Remove the dough from the bowl and begin to knead it, working in the remaining flour a little at a time. Knead for 8–10 minutes. By the end the dough should be elastic and smooth. Form it into a ball.

4 Lightly oil a mixing bowl. Place the dough in the bowl. Stretch a damp dish towel or clear film across the top of the bowl, and leave it to stand in a warm place until the dough has doubled in volume, about 40–50 minutes or more, depending on the type of yeast used. To test whether the dough has risen enough, poke two fingers into the dough. If the indentations remain, the dough is ready to use.

5 ▲ Punch the dough down with your fist to release the air. Knead for 1–2 minutes.

6 ▲ Brush a tin with oil. Press the dough into the tin with your fingers to a layer 2 cm/1 inch thick. Cover and leave to rise for 30 minutes. Preheat the oven. Make indentations all over the focaccia with your fingers. Brush with oil, add filling and bake until pale golden brown.

7 ▲ For bread sticks: There's no need for the first rising. Divide dough into walnut-size pieces and roll out on a floured surface with your hands, into thin sausage shapes. Transfer to a greased baking tray, cover and leave in a warm place for 10–15 minutes. Bake until crisp.

MAKING SCONES AND POPOVERS

Scones are quick breads made with a soft dough based on flour and milk with a raising agent added. The dough may be rolled out and cut into shapes, or it may be dropped from a spoon onto a baking sheet, or lightly patted out and then stamped out with a cutter into rounds or other shapes.

Popovers are individual batter puddings, made in a similar way to Yorkshire puddings, then flavoured.

1 For scones: Sift together the dry ingredients into a large mixing bowl (flour, baking powder with or without bicarbonate of soda, salt, sugar, spices, etc).

2 ▲ Add the fat (butter, margarine, or vegetable fat). With a pastry blender or two knives, cut the fat into the dry ingredients until the mixture resembles fine crumbs, or rub in the fat with your fingertips.

3 ▲ Add the liquid ingredients (milk, cream, buttermilk, eggs). Stir with a fork until the dry ingredients are thoroughly moistened and will come together in a ball of fairly soft dough in the centre of the bowl.

4 ▲ Turn the dough on to a lightly floured surface. Knead it very lightly, folding and pressing, to mix evenly, about 30 seconds. Roll or pat out the dough to 2 cm (1 in) thickness.

5 ▲ With a floured, sharp-edged cutter, cut out rounds or other shapes. Arrange on an ungreased baking sheet. Brush with beaten egg or cream. Bake until golden brown. Serve immediately.

6 ▲ For griddle scones: If using a well-seasoned cast iron griddle, there is no need to grease it. Heat it slowly and evenly. Put scone triangles or rounds on the hot griddle and cook for 4–5 minutes on each side or until golden brown and cooked through.

1 For popovers: Sift the flour into a large bowl along with other dry ingredients such as salt and ground black pepper. Make a well in the centre of dry ingredients and put in the eggs, egg yolks and some of the liquid.

2 With a wooden spoon, beat together the eggs and liquid in the well just to mix them. Gradually draw in some of the flour from the sides, stirring vigorously.

3 When the mixture is smooth, stir in the remaining liquid. Stir just until the ingredients are combined – the trick is not to overmix.

4 ▲ Pour the mixture into greased muffin tins or ramekins and bake until golden brown. Do not open the oven door during baking time or the popovers may collapse. Run a knife around the edge of each popover to loosen, then turn out and serve hot.

Cutting Tips for Scones
- Be sure the cutter or knife is sharp so that the edges of the scone shapes are not compressed; this would prevent rising.
- Cut the shapes close together so that you won't have to re-roll the dough more than once.
- If necessary, a short, sturdy drinking glass can be pressed into service as a cutter. Flour the rim well and do not press too hard.
- While cutting out, don't twist the cutter.

SWEET MUFFINS

Golden, moist muffins fresh from the oven are a
wonderful way to start the day and Cherry Marmalade
Muffins make an unusual breakfast treat. Enjoy them at
teatime, too, or whenever you feel like a delicious snack.
The recipes here are flavoured with a tempting variety
of fresh and dried fruits, nuts and chocolate.

Prune Muffins

1 egg

8 fl oz (250 ml) milk

4 fl oz (125 ml) vegetable oil

1¾ oz (50 g) caster sugar

1 oz (30 g) dark brown sugar

10 oz (285 g) plain flour

2 teaspoons baking powder

½ teaspoon salt

¼ teaspoon grated nutmeg

4 oz (115 g) cooked stoned prunes, chopped

1 Preheat a 400°F/200°C/Gas 6 oven. Grease a 12-cup muffin tin.

2 Break the egg into a mixing bowl and beat with a fork. Beat in the milk and oil.

3 ▼ Stir in the sugars. Set aside.

4 Sift the flour, baking powder, salt and nutmeg into a mixing bowl. Make a well in the centre, pour in the egg mixture and stir until moistened. Do not overmix; the batter should be slightly lumpy.

5 ▲ Fold in the prunes.

6 Fill the prepared cups two-thirds full. Bake until golden brown, about 20 minutes. Let stand 10 minutes before turning out. Serve warm or at room temperature.

Yogurt and Honey Muffins

2 oz (55 g) butter

5 tablespoons clear honey

8 fl oz (250 ml) plain yogurt

1 large egg, at room temperature

grated rind of 1 lemon

2 fl oz (65 ml) lemon juice

5 oz (140 g) plain flour

6 oz (170 g) wholemeal flour

1½ teaspoons bicarbonate of soda

⅛ teaspoon grated nutmeg

~ **VARIATION** ~

For Walnut Yogurt Honey Muffins, add 2 oz (55 g) chopped walnuts, folded in with the flour. This makes a more substantial muffin.

1 Preheat a 375°F/190°C/Gas 5 oven. Grease a 12-cup muffin tin or use paper cases.

2 In a saucepan, melt the butter and honey. Remove from the heat and set aside to cool slightly.

3 ▲ In a bowl, whisk together the yogurt, egg, lemon rind and juice. Add the butter and honey mixture. Set aside.

4 ▲ In another bowl, sift together the dry ingredients.

5 Fold the dry ingredients into the yogurt mixture to blend.

6 Fill the prepared cups two-thirds full. Bake until the tops spring back when touched lightly, 20–25 minutes. Let cool in the tin for 5 minutes before turning out. Serve warm or at room temperature.

Blueberry Muffins

MAKES 12

6¼ oz (180 g) plain flour

2¼ oz (60 g) sugar

2 teaspoons baking powder

¼ teaspoon salt

2 eggs

2 oz (55 g) butter, melted

6 fl oz (175 ml) milk

1 teaspoon vanilla essence

1 teaspoon grated lemon rind

6 oz (170 g) fresh blueberries

1 Preheat a 400°F/200°C/Gas 6 oven.

2 ▼ Grease a 12-cup muffin tin or use paper cases.

3 ▲ Sift the flour, sugar, baking powder and salt into a bowl.

4 In another bowl, whisk the eggs until blended. Add the melted butter, milk, vanilla and lemon rind and stir to combine.

5 Make a well in the dry ingredients and pour in the egg mixture. With a large metal spoon, stir just until the flour is moistened, not until smooth.

6 ▲ Fold in the blueberries.

7 ▲ Spoon the batter into the cups, leaving room for the muffins to rise.

8 Bake until the tops spring back when touched lightly, 20–25 minutes. Let cool in the pan for 5 minutes before turning out.

Apple and Cranberry Muffins

Makes 12

2 oz (55 g) butter or margarine
1 egg
3½ oz (100 g) sugar
grated rind of 1 large orange
4 fl oz (125 ml) freshly squeezed orange juice
5 oz (140 g) plain flour
1 teaspoon baking powder
½ teaspoon bicarbonate of soda
1 teaspoon ground cinnamon
½ teaspoon grated nutmeg
½ teaspoon ground allspice
¼ teaspoon ground ginger
¼ teaspoon salt
1–2 dessert apples
6 oz (170 g) cranberries
2 oz (55 g) walnuts, chopped
icing sugar, for dusting (optional)

1 Preheat the oven to 350°F/180°C/ Gas 4. Grease a 12-cup muffin tin or use paper cases.

2 Melt the butter or margarine over gentle heat. Set aside to cool.

3 ▲ Place the egg in a mixing bowl and whisk lightly. Add the melted butter or margarine and whisk to combine.

4 Add the sugar, orange rind and juice. Whisk to blend, then set aside.

5 In a large bowl, sift together the flour, baking powder, bicarbonate of soda, cinnamon, nutmeg, allspice, ginger and salt. Set aside.

6 ▲ Quarter, core and peel the apples. With a sharp knife, chop coarsely.

7 Make a well in the dry ingredients and pour in the egg mixture. With a spoon, stir until just blended.

8 ▲ Add the apples, cranberries and walnuts and stir to blend.

9 Fill the cups three-quarters full and bake until the tops spring back when touched lightly, 25–30 minutes. Transfer to a rack to cool. Dust with icing sugar, if desired.

Chocolate Chip Muffins

MAKES 10

4 oz (115 g) butter or margarine, at room temperature

2½ oz (70 g) caster sugar

1 oz (30 g) dark brown sugar

2 eggs, at room temperature

7½ oz (215 g) plain flour

1 teaspoon baking powder

4 fl oz (125 ml) milk

6 oz (170 g) plain chocolate chips

1 Preheat the oven to 375°F/190°C/ Gas 5. Grease 10 muffin cups or use paper cases.

2 ▼ With an electric mixer, cream the butter until soft. Add both sugars and beat until light and fluffy. Beat in the eggs, 1 at a time.

3 Sift together the flour and baking powder, twice. Fold into the butter mixture, alternating with the milk.

4 ▲ Divide half the mixture between the muffin cups. Sprinkle several chocolate chips on top, then cover with a spoonful of the batter. To ensure even baking, half-fill any empty cups with water.

5 Bake until lightly coloured, about 25 minutes. Let stand 5 minutes before turning out.

Chocolate Walnut Muffins

MAKES 12

6 oz (170 g) unsalted butter

5 oz (140 g) plain chocolate

7 oz (200 g) caster sugar

2 oz (55 g) dark brown sugar

4 eggs

1 teaspoon vanilla essence

¼ teaspoon almond essence

3¾ oz (110 g) plain flour

1 tablespoon unsweetened cocoa powder

4 oz (115 g) walnuts, chopped

1 Preheat the oven to 350°F/180°C/ Gas 4. Grease a 12-cup muffin pan or use paper cases.

2 ▼ Melt the butter with the chocolate in the top of a double boiler or in a heatproof bowl set over a pan of hot water. Transfer to a large mixing bowl.

3 Stir both the sugars into the chocolate mixture. Mix in the eggs, 1 at a time, then add the vanilla and almond essences.

4 Sift over the flour and cocoa.

5 ▲ Fold in and stir in the walnuts.

6 Fill the prepared cups almost to the top and bake until a skewer inserted in the centre barely comes out clean, 30–35 minutes. Let stand 5 minutes before turning out onto a rack to cool completely.

Raisin Bran Muffins

MAKES 15

2 oz (55 g) butter or margarine

1½ oz (45 g) plain flour

2 oz (55 g) wholewheat flour

1½ teaspoons bicarbonate of soda

⅛ teaspoon salt

1 teaspoon ground cinnamon

1 oz (30 g) bran

3 oz (85 g) raisins

2½ oz (65 g) dark brown sugar

2 oz (55 g) caster sugar

1 egg

8 fl oz (250 ml) buttermilk

juice of ½ lemon

1 Preheat a 400°F/200°C/Gas 6 oven. Grease 15 deep muffin tins.

2 ▲ Place the butter or margarine in a saucepan and melt over gentle heat. Set aside.

3 In a mixing bowl, sift together the flours, bicarbonate of soda, salt and cinnamon.

4 ▲ Add the bran, raisins and sugars and stir until blended.

5 In another bowl, mix together the egg, buttermilk, lemon juice and melted butter.

6 ▲ Add the buttermilk mixture to the dry ingredients and stir lightly and quickly just until moistened; do not mix until smooth.

7 ▲ Spoon the mixture into the prepared muffin tins, filling the cups almost to the top. Half-fill any empty cups with water.

8 Bake until golden, 15–20 minutes. Serve warm or at room temperature.

Raspberry Crumble Muffins

MAKES 12

6 oz (170 g) plain flour
2 oz (55 g) caster sugar
1¾ oz (50 g) light brown sugar
2 teaspoons baking powder
⅛ teaspoon salt
1 teaspoon ground cinnamon
4 oz (115 g) butter, melted
1 egg
4 fl oz (125 ml) milk
5 oz (140 g) fresh raspberries
grated rind of 1 lemon

FOR THE CRUMBLE TOPPING

1 oz (30 g) finely chopped pecans or walnuts
2 oz (55 g) dark brown sugar
3 tablespoons plain flour
1 teaspoon ground cinnamon
3 tablespoons butter, melted

1 Preheat a 350°F/180°C/Gas 4 oven. Grease 12 deep muffin tins or use paper cases.

2 Sift the flour into a bowl. Add the sugars, baking powder, salt and cinnamon and stir to blend.

3 ▲ Make a well in the centre. Place the butter, egg and milk in the well and mix until just combined. Stir in the raspberries and lemon rind. Spoon the mixture into the prepared tins, filling the cups almost to the top.

4 ▼ For the crumble topping, mix the nuts, dark brown sugar, flour and cinnamon in a bowl. Add the melted butter and stir to blend.

5 ▲ Spoon some of the crumble over each bun. Bake until browned, about 25 minutes. Transfer to a rack to cool slightly. Serve warm.

Carrot Muffins

MAKES 12

6 oz (170 g) margarine, at room temperature

3½ oz (100 g) dark brown sugar

1 egg, at room temperature

1 tbsp water

8 oz (225 g) carrots, grated

5 oz (140 g) plain flour

1 tsp baking powder

½ tsp bicarbonate of soda

1 tsp ground cinnamon

¼ tsp grated nutmeg

½ tsp salt

1 Preheat a 350°F/180°C/Gas 4 oven. Grease a 12-cup bun tray or use paper cases.

2 With an electric mixer, cream the margarine and sugar until light and fluffy. Beat in the egg and water.

3 ▲ Stir in the carrots.

4 Sift over the flour, baking powder, bicarbonate of soda, cinnamon, nutmeg and salt. Stir to blend.

5 ▼ Spoon the mixture into the prepared bun tray, filling the cups almost to the top. Bake until the tops spring back when touched lightly, about 35 minutes. Let stand 10 minutes before transferring to a rack.

Dried Cherry Muffins

MAKES 16

8 fl oz (250 ml) plain yoghurt

6 oz (170 g) dried cherries

4 oz (115 g) butter, at room temperature

6 oz (170 g) caster sugar

2 eggs, at room temperature

1 tsp vanilla essence

7 oz (200 g) plain flour

2 tsp baking powder

1 tsp bicarbonate of soda

⅛ tsp salt

1 In a mixing bowl, combine the yoghurt and cherries. Cover and let stand for 30 minutes.

2 Preheat a 350°F/180°C/Gas 4 oven. Grease 16 bun-tray cups or use paper cases.

3 With an electric mixer, cream the butter and sugar together until light and fluffy.

4 ▼ Add the eggs, 1 at a time, beating well after each addition. Add the vanilla and the cherry mixture and stir to blend. Set aside.

5 ▲ In another bowl, sift together the flour, baking powder, bicarbonate soda and salt. Fold into the cherry mixture in 3 batches.

6 Fill the prepared cups two-thirds full. For even baking, half-fill any empty cups with water. Bake until the tops spring back when touched lightly, about 20 minutes. Transfer to a rack to cool.

Banana Muffins

MAKES 10

9 oz (250 g) plain flour
1 teaspoon baking powder
1 teaspoon bicarbonate of soda
¼ teaspoon salt
½ teaspoon ground cinnamon
¼ teaspoon grated nutmeg
3 large ripe bananas
1 egg
2½ oz (70 g) dark brown sugar
2 fl oz (50 ml) vegetable oil
1 oz (30 g) raisins

1 ▼ Preheat the oven to 375°F/ 190°C/Gas 5. Lightly grease or line 10 deep muffin tins with paper cases.

2 Sift together the flour, baking powder, bicarbonate of soda, salt, cinnamon and nutmeg. Set aside.

3 ▲ With an electric mixer, beat the peeled bananas at moderate speed until mashed.

4 ▲ Beat in the egg, sugar and oil.

5 Add the dry ingredients and beat in gradually, on low speed. Mix just until blended. With a wooden spoon, stir in the raisins.

6 Fill the prepared cups two-thirds full. For even baking, half-fill any empty cups with water.

7 ▲ Bake until the tops spring back when touched lightly, 20–25 minutes. Transfer to a rack to cool.

Maple Pecan Muffins

MAKES 20

6 oz (170 g) pecans
12 oz (340 g) flour
1 teaspoon baking powder
1 teaspoon bicarbonate of soda
¼ teaspoon salt
¼ teaspoon ground cinnamon
3½ oz (100 g) caster sugar
2½ oz (70 g) light brown sugar
3 tablespoons maple syrup
5 oz (150 g) butter, at room temperature
3 eggs, at room temperature
½ pint (300 ml) buttermilk
60 pecan halves, for decorating

1 Preheat the oven to 350°F/180°C/ Gas 4. Lightly grease 24 deep muffin tins or use paper cases.

2 ▲ Spread the pecans on a baking sheet and toast in the oven for 5 minutes. When cool, chop coarsely and set aside.

3 In a bowl, sift together the flour, baking powder, bicarbonate of soda, salt and cinnamon. Set aside.

4 ▲ In a large mixing bowl, combine the caster sugar, light brown sugar, maple syrup and butter. Beat with an electric mixer until light and fluffy.

5 Add the eggs, 1 at a time, beating to incorporate thoroughly after each addition.

6 ▲ Pour half the buttermilk and half the dry ingredients into the butter mixture, then stir until blended. Repeat with the remaining buttermilk and dry ingredients.

7 Fold in the chopped pecans. Fill the prepared cups two-thirds full. Top with the pecan halves. For even baking, half-fill any empty cups with water.

8 Bake until puffed up and golden, 20–25 minutes. Let stand 5 minutes before unmoulding.

~ **VARIATION** ~

For Pecan Spice Muffins, substitute an equal quantity of golden syrup for the maple syrup. Increase the cinnamon to ½ teaspoon, and add 1 teaspoon ground ginger and ½ teaspoon grated nutmeg, sifted with the dry ingredients.

Oat and Raisin Muffins

MAKES 12

3 oz (85 g) rolled oats
8 fl oz (250 ml) buttermilk
4 oz (120 g) butter, at room temperature
3½ oz (100 g) dark brown sugar
1 egg, at room temperature
4 oz (120 g) flour
1 teaspoon baking powder
½ teaspoon bicarbonate of soda
¼ teaspoon salt
1 oz (30 g) raisins

~ COOK'S TIP ~

If buttermilk is not available, add 1 teaspoon lemon juice or vinegar to the milk. Let the mixture stand for a few minutes to curdle.

1 ▲ In a bowl, combine the oats and buttermilk and let soak for 1 hour.

2 ▲ Lightly grease a 12-cup muffin tin or use paper cases.

3 ▲ Preheat the oven to 400°F/ 200°C/Gas 6. With an electric mixer, cream the butter and sugar until light and fluffy. Beat in the egg.

4 In another bowl, sift the flour, baking powder, bicarbonate of soda and salt. Stir into the butter mixture, alternating with the oat mixture. Fold in the raisins. Do not overmix.

5 Fill the prepared cups two-thirds full. Bake until a skewer inserted in the centre comes out clean, 20–25 minutes. Transfer to a rack to cool.

Pumpkin Muffins

MAKES 14

4 oz (120 g) butter or margarine, at room temperature
5 oz (150 g) dark brown sugar
4 tablespoons molasses
1 egg, at room temperature, beaten
8 oz (225 g) cooked or canned pumpkin
8 oz (225 g) flour
¼ teaspoon salt
1 teaspoon bicarbonate of soda
1½ teaspoons ground cinnamon
1 teaspoon grated nutmeg
1 oz (30 g) currants or raisins

1 Preheat the oven to 400°F/200°C/ Gas 6. Grease 14 muffin cups or use paper cases.

2 With an electric mixer, cream the butter or margarine until soft. Add the sugar and molasses and beat until light and fluffy.

3 ▲ Add the egg and pumpkin and stir until well blended.

4 Sift over the flour, salt, bicarbonate of soda, cinnamon and nutmeg. Fold just enough to blend; do not overmix.

5 ▼ Fold in the currants or raisins.

6 Spoon the mixture into the prepared muffin cups, filling them three-quarters full.

7 Bake until the tops spring back when touched lightly, 12–15 minutes. Serve warm or cold.

Blackberry and Almond Muffins

MAKES 12

11 oz (300 g) plain flour
2 oz (50 g) light brown sugar
4 teaspoons baking powder
pinch of salt
2¼ oz (60 g) chopped blanched almonds
3½ oz (100 g) fresh blackberries
2 eggs
7 fl oz (200 ml) milk
4 tablespoons melted butter, plus a little more to grease cups, if using
1 tablespoon sloe gin
1 tablespoon rosewater

1 ▼ Mix the flour, sugar, baking powder and salt in a bowl and stir in the almonds and blackberries, mixing them well to coat with the flour mixture. Preheat the oven to 400°F/200°C/Gas 6.

2 ▲ In another bowl, mix the eggs with the milk, then gradually add the butter, sloe gin and rosewater. Make a well in the centre of the bowl of dry ingredients and add the egg and milk mixture. Stir well.

3 Lightly grease 12 deep muffin tins. Spoon in the mixture and bake for 20–25 minutes or until browned. Turn out the muffins on to a wire rack to cool. Serve with butter.

~ COOK'S TIP ~

Other berries can be substituted for the blackberries, such as elderberries or blueberries.

~ VARIATION ~

For Blackberry and Apple Muffins, substitute 2 dessert apples, peeled, cored and diced for the almonds. All 1 teaspoon ground coriander to the flour mixture, and instead of the sloe gin and rosewater, substitute 2 tablespoons of Crème de Mûre.

Cherry Marmalade Muffins

MAKES 12

8 oz (225 g) self-raising flour
1 teaspoon mixed spice
3 oz (85 g) caster sugar
4 oz (120 g) glacé cherries, quartered
2 tablespoons orange marmalade
¼ pint (150 ml) skimmed milk
2 oz (55 g) soft sunflower margarine
marmalade, to brush

1 ▲ Preheat the oven to 400°F/200°C/Gas 6. Lightly grease 12 deep muffin tins with oil.

2 ▲ Sift together the flour and spice then stir in the sugar and cherries.

3 Mix the marmalade with the milk and beat into the dry ingredients with the margarine. Spoon into the greased tins. Bake for 20–25 minutes, until golden brown and firm.

4 ▼ Turn out on to a wire rack and brush the tops with warmed marmalade. Serve warm or cold.

~ **VARIATION** ~

To make Honey, Nut and Lemon Muffins, substitute 2 tablespoons clear honey for the orange marmalade, and the juice and finely grated rind of a lemon, and 2 oz (55 g) toasted, chopped hazelnuts, instead of the glacé cherries.

Banana and Pecan Muffins

MAKES 8

5 oz (150 g) plain flour

1½ teaspoons baking powder

2 oz (55 g) butter or margarine, at room temperature

5 oz (150 g) caster sugar

1 egg

1 teaspoon vanilla essence

3 medium bananas, mashed

2 oz (55 g) pecans, chopped

5 tablespoons milk

1 Preheat the oven to 375°F/190°C/ Gas 5. Lightly grease 8 deep muffin tins.

2 Sift the flour and baking powder into a small bowl. Set aside.

3 ▲ With an electric mixer, cream the butter or margarine and sugar together. Add the egg and vanilla and beat until fluffy. Mix in the banana.

4 ▼ Add the pecans. With the mixer on low speed, beat in the flour mixture alternately with the milk.

5 Spoon the mixture into the prepared muffin cups, filling them two-thirds full. Bake until golden brown and a skewer inserted into the centre of a muffin comes out clean, 20–25 minutes.

6 Let cool in the tin on a wire rack for 10 minutes. To loosen, run a knife gently around each muffin and unmould on to the wire rack. Let cool 10 minutes longer before serving.

~ VARIATION ~

Use an equal quantity of walnuts instead of the pecans.

Blueberry and Cinnamon Muffins

MAKES 8

4 oz (120 g) plain flour

1 tablespoon baking powder

pinch of salt

2½ oz (70 g) light brown sugar

1 egg

6 fl oz (175 ml) milk

3 tablespoons vegetable oil

2 teaspoons ground cinnamon

4 oz (120 g) fresh or thawed frozen blueberries

1 Preheat the oven to 375°F/190°C/ Gas 5. Lightly grease 8 deep muffin tins.

2 With an electric mixer, beat the first 8 ingredients together until smooth.

3 ▲ Fold in the blueberries.

4 ▲ Spoon the mixture into the muffin cups, filling them two-thirds full. Bake until a skewer inserted in the centre of a muffin comes out clean, about 25 minutes.

5 Let cool in the tins on a wire rack for 10 minutes, then unmould the muffins on to the wire rack and allow to cool completely.

Raspberry Muffins

MAKES 10–12

4 oz (120 g) self-raising flour

4 oz (120 g) wholemeal self-raising flour

3 tablespoons caster sugar

½ teaspoon salt

2 eggs, beaten

7 fl oz (200 ml) milk

2 oz (55 g) butter, melted

6 oz (170 g) raspberries, fresh or frozen (defrosted for less than 30 minutes)

1 ▼ Preheat the oven to 375°F/ 190°C/Gas 5. Lightly grease the muffin tins, or use paper cases. Sift the dry ingredients together, then tip back in the wholewheat flakes from the sieve.

2 ▲ Beat the eggs, milk and butter with the dry ingredients to give a thick batter. Add the raspberries.

3 ▲ Stir in the raspberries gently. (If you are using frozen raspberries, work quickly as the cold berries make the mixture solidify.) If you mix too much the raspberries begin to disintegrate and colour the dough. Spoon the mixture into the tins or paper cases.

4 Bake the muffins for 30 minutes, until well risen and just firm. Serve warm or cool.

Blueberry and Vanilla Muffins

MAKES 12

12 oz (340 g) plain flour
2 teaspoons baking powder
¼ teaspoon salt
4 oz (120 g) caster sugar
2 eggs, beaten
½ pint (300 ml) milk
4 oz (120 g) butter, melted
1 teaspoon vanilla essence
6 oz (170 g) blueberries

1 Preheat the oven to 400°F/200°C/ Gas 6. Lightly grease 12 deep muffin tins.

2 Sift the flour, baking powder and salt into a large mixing bowl and stir in the sugar.

3 ▲ Place the eggs, milk, butter and vanilla essence in a separate bowl and whisk together well.

~ **COOK'S TIP** ~

Fresh blueberries are best for this recipe, but if you can't find them, use frozen blueberries instead. Just add them to the batter without thawing first.

4 ▲ Fold the egg mixture into the dry ingredients with a metal spoon, then gently stir in the blueberries.

5 Spoon the mixture into the muffin cups, filling them until just below the top. Place the muffin tin on the top shelf of the oven and bake for 20–25 minutes, until the muffins are well risen and lightly browned. Leave the muffins in the tin for 5 minutes and then turn them out on to a wire rack to cool. Serve warm or cold.

SWEET
QUICK BREADS

When there's no time to make yeasted bread, baking
quick breads can be equally satisfying. Old favourites
include Banana and Oat Gingerbread, or try the more
unusual Sweet Potato and Raisin Bread, or Courgette
and Walnut Loaf. These versatile breads can be
served with fresh fruit for an unusual dessert,
or just toasted and spread with butter and jam.

Wholewheat Banana Nut Loaf

MAKES 1 LOAF

4 oz (115 g) butter, at room temperature

4 oz (115 g) caster sugar

2 eggs, at room temperature

4 oz (115 g) plain flour

1 teaspoon bicarbonate of soda

⅛ teaspoon salt

1 teaspoon ground cinnamon

2 oz (55 g) wholewheat flour

3 large ripe bananas

1 teaspoon vanilla essence

2 oz (55 g) chopped walnuts

1 Preheat a 350°F/180°C/Gas 4 oven. Line the bottom and sides of a 9 × 5 in (23 × 13 cm) loaf tin with greaseproof paper and grease the paper.

2 With an electric mixer, cream the butter and sugar together until light and fluffy.

3 ▲ Add the eggs, 1 at a time, beating well after each addition.

4 Sift the plain flour, bicarbonate of soda, salt and cinnamon over the butter mixture and stir to blend.

5 ▲ Stir in the wholewheat flour.

6 ▲ With a fork, mash the bananas to a purée, then stir into the mixture. Stir in the vanilla and nuts.

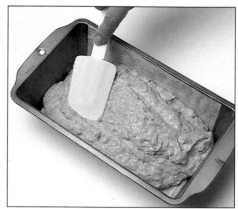

7 ▲ Pour the mixture into the prepared tin and spread level.

8 Bake until a skewer inserted in the centre comes out clean, 50–60 minutes. Let stand 10 minutes before transferring to a rack.

Sweet Potato and Raisin Bread

MAKES 1 LOAF

12 oz (340 g) flour
2 teaspoons baking powder
½ teaspoon salt
1 teaspoon ground cinnamon
½ teaspoon grated nutmeg
1 lb (450 g) mashed cooked sweet potatoes
3½ oz (100 g) light brown sugar
4 oz (120 g) butter or margarine, melted and cooled
3 eggs, beaten
3 oz (85 g) raisins

1 ▼ Preheat the oven to 350°F/ 180°C/Gas 4. Grease a 2 lb (900 g) loaf dish or tin.

2 Sift the flour, baking powder, salt, cinnamon, and nutmeg into a small bowl. Set aside.

3 ▼ With an electric mixer, beat the mashed sweet potatoes with the brown sugar, butter or margarine, and eggs until well mixed.

4 ▼ Add the flour mixture and the raisins. Stir with a wooden spoon until the flour is just mixed in.

5 ▲ Transfer the batter to the prepared dish or tin. Bake until a cake tester inserted in the centre comes out clean, 1–1¼ hours.

6 Let cool in the pan on a wire rack for 15 minutes, then unmould the bread from the dish or tin onto the wire rack and let cool completely.

Courgette and Walnut Loaf

MAKES 1 LOAF

3 eggs
3 oz (85 g) light muscovado sugar
4 fl oz (125 ml) sunflower oil
8 oz (225 g) wholemeal flour
1 teaspoon baking powder
1 teaspoon bicarbonate of soda
1 teaspoon ground cinnamon
¾ teaspoon ground allspice
½ teaspoon green cardamoms, seeds removed and crushed
5 oz (150 g) courgettes, coarsely grated
4 oz (120 g) walnuts, chopped
2 oz (55 g) sunflower seeds

1 ▲ Preheat the oven to 350°F/ 180°C/Gas 4. Line the base and sides of a 2 lb (900 g) loaf tin with non-stick baking paper.

2 ▲ Beat the eggs and sugar together and gradually add the oil.

3 ▲ Sift the flour into a bowl together with the baking powder, bicarbonate of soda, cinnamon and allspice.

4 ▲ Mix into the egg mixture with the rest of the ingredients, reserving 1 tablespoon of the sunflower seeds for the top.

5 ▲ Spoon into the loaf tin, level off the top, and sprinkle with the reserved sunflower seeds.

6 ▲ Bake for 1 hour or until a skewer inserted in the centre comes out clean. Leave to cool slightly before turning out onto a wire rack to cool completely.

~ VARIATION ~

To make Spinach Loaf, use 4 oz (120 g) chopped, cooked spinach instead of the courgettes. Substitute ¼ teaspoon freshly grated nutmeg for the cardamoms, and sesame seeds for the sunflower seeds. Stir in 2 oz (55 g) grated Parmesan or Cheddar cheese.

Cranberry and Orange Bread

MAKES 1 LOAF

8 oz (225 g) plain flour

4 oz (115 g) caster sugar

1 tablespoon baking powder

½ teaspoon salt

grated rind of 1 large orange

5½ fl oz (170 ml) fresh orange juice

2 eggs, lightly beaten

3 oz (85 g) butter or margarine, melted

4 oz (115 g) fresh cranberries, or
   bilberries

2 oz (55 g) chopped walnuts

1 Preheat a 350°F/180°C/Gas 4 oven. Line a 9 × 5 in (23 × 13 cm) loaf tin with greaseproof paper and grease.

2 Sift the flour, sugar, baking powder and salt into a mixing bowl.

3 ▼ Stir in the orange rind.

4 ▲ Make a well in the centre and add the orange juice, eggs and melted butter or margarine. Stir from the centre until the ingredients are blended; do not overmix.

5 ▲ Add the berries and walnuts and stir until blended.

6 Transfer the mixture to the prepared tin and bake until a skewer inserted in the centre comes out clean, 45–50 minutes.

7 ▲ Let cool in the tin for 10 minutes before transferring to a rack to cool completely. Serve thinly sliced, toasted or plain, with butter or cream cheese and jam.

Date and Pecan Loaf

MAKES 1 LOAF

6 oz (170 g) stoned dates, chopped
6 fl oz (175 ml) boiling water
2 oz (55 g) unsalted butter, at room temperature
2 oz (55 g) dark brown sugar
2 oz (55 g) caster sugar
1 egg, at room temperature
2 tablespoons brandy
5½ oz (165 g) plain flour
2 tsp baking powder
½ teaspoon salt
¾ teaspoon freshly grated nutmeg
3 oz (85 g) coarsely chopped pecans or walnuts

1 ▲ Place the dates in a bowl and pour over the boiling water. Set aside to cool.

2 Preheat a 350°F/180°C/Gas 4 oven. Line a 9 × 5 in (23 × 13 cm) loaf tin with greaseproof paper and grease.

3 ▲ With an electric mixer, cream the butter and sugars until light and fluffy. Beat in the egg and brandy, then set aside.

4 Sift the flour, baking powder, salt and nutmeg together, 3 times.

5 ▼ Fold the dry ingredients into the sugar mixture in 3 batches, alternating with the dates and water.

6 ▲ Fold in the nuts.

7 Pour the mixture into the prepared tin and bake until a skewer inserted in the centre comes out clean, 45–50 minutes. Let cool in the tin for 10 minutes before transferring to a rack to cool completely.

Blueberry Crumble Tea Bread

MAKES 8 PIECES

2 oz (55 g) butter or margarine, at room temperature

6 oz (170 g) caster sugar

1 egg, at room temperature

4 fl oz (125 ml) milk

8 oz (225 g) plain flour

2 teaspoons baking powder

½ teaspoon salt

10 oz (285 g) fresh blueberries, or bilberries

FOR THE TOPPING

4 oz (115 g) sugar

1½ oz (45 g) plain flour

½ teaspoon ground cinnamon

2 oz (55 g) butter, cut in pieces

1 Preheat a 375°F/190°C/Gas 5 oven. Grease a 9 in (23 cm) baking dish.

2 With an electric mixer, cream the butter or margarine with the sugar until light and fluffy. Add the egg, beat to combine, then mix in the milk until blended.

3 ▼ Sift over the flour, baking powder and salt and stir just enough to blend the ingredients.

4 ▲ Add the berries and stir.

5 Transfer to the baking dish.

6 ▲ For the topping, place the sugar, flour, cinnamon and butter in a mixing bowl. Cut in with a pastry blender until the mixture resembles coarse breadcrumbs.

7 ▲ Sprinkle the topping over the mixture in the baking dish.

8 Bake until a skewer inserted in the centre comes out clean, about 45 minutes. Serve warm or cold.

Dried Fruit Loaf

MAKES 1 LOAF

1 lb (450 g) mixed dried fruit, such as currants, raisins, chopped dried apricots and dried cherries
10 fl oz (300 ml) cold strong tea
7 oz (200 g) dark brown sugar
grated rind and juice of 1 small orange
grated rind and juice of 1 lemon
1 egg, lightly beaten
7 oz (200 g) plain flour
1 tablespoon baking powder
⅛ teaspoon salt

1 ▲ In a bowl, mix the dried fruit with the tea and soak overnight.

2 Preheat a 350°F/180°C/Gas 4 oven. Line the bottom and sides of a 9 × 5 in (23 × 13 cm) loaf tin with greaseproof paper and grease the paper.

3 ▲ Strain the fruit, reserving the liquid. In a bowl, combine the sugar, orange and lemon rind, and fruit.

4 ▼ Pour the orange and lemon juice into a measuring jug; if the quantity is less than 8 fl oz (250 ml), top up with the soaking liquid.

5 Stir the citrus juices and egg into the dried fruit mixture.

6 In another bowl, sift together the flour, baking powder and salt. Stir into the fruit mixture until blended.

7 Transfer to the prepared tin and bake until a skewer inserted in the centre comes out clean, about 1¼ hours. Let stand 10 minutes before unmoulding.

Lemon and Walnut Tea Bread

MAKES 1 LOAF

4 oz (115 g) butter or margarine, at room temperature
3½ oz (100 g) sugar
2 eggs, at room temperature, separated
grated rind of 2 lemons
2 tablespoons lemon juice
7½ oz (215 g) plain flour
2 teaspoons baking powder
4 fl oz (125 ml) milk
2 oz (55 g) walnuts, chopped
⅛ teaspoon salt

1 Preheat a 350°F/180°C/Gas 4 oven. Line a 9 × 5 in (23 × 13 cm) loaf tin with greaseproof paper and grease.

2 With an electric mixer, cream the butter or margarine with the sugar until light and fluffy.

3 ▲ Beat in the egg yolks.

4 Add the lemon rind and juice and stir until blended. Set aside.

5 ▲ In another bowl, sift together the flour and baking powder, 3 times. Fold into the butter mixture in 3 batches, alternating with the milk. Fold in the walnuts. Set aside.

6 ▲ Beat the egg whites and salt until stiff peaks form. Fold a large dollop of the egg whites into the walnut mixture to lighten it. Fold in the remaining egg whites carefully until just blended.

7 ▲ Pour the batter into the prepared tin and bake until a skewer inserted in the centre of the loaf comes out clean, 45–50 minutes. Let stand 5 minutes before turning out onto a rack to cool completely.

Apricot Nut Loaf

MAKES 1 LOAF

4 oz (115 g) dried apricots
1 large orange
3 oz (85 g) raisins
5 oz (140 g) caster sugar
3 fl oz (85 ml) oil
2 eggs, lightly beaten
9 oz (250 g) plain flour
2 teaspoons baking powder
½ teaspoon salt
1 teaspoon bicarbonate of soda
2 oz (55 g) chopped walnuts

1 Preheat a 350°F/180°C/Gas 4 oven. Line a 9 × 5 in (23 × 13 cm) loaf tin with greaseproof paper and grease.

2 Place the apricots in a bowl, cover with lukewarm water and leave to stand for 30 minutes.

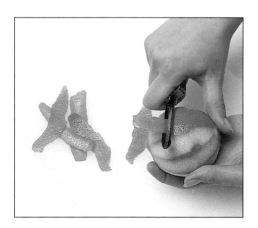

3 ▲ With a vegetable peeler, remove the orange rind, leaving the pith.

4 With a sharp knife, finely chop the orange rind strips.

5 Drain the apricots and chop coarsely. Place in a bowl with the orange rind and raisins. Set aside.

6 Squeeze the peeled orange. Measure the juice and add enough hot water to obtain 6 fl oz (175 ml) liquid.

7 ▼ Pour the orange juice mixture over the apricot mixture. Stir in the sugar, oil and eggs. Set aside.

8 In another bowl, sift together the flour, baking powder, salt and bicarbonate of soda. Fold the flour mixture into the apricot mixture in 3 batches.

9 ▲ Stir in the walnuts.

10 Spoon the mixture into the prepared tin and bake until a skewer inserted in the centre comes out clean, 55–60 minutes. If the loaf browns too quickly, protect the top with a sheet of foil. Let cool in the pan for 10 minutes before transferring to a rack to cool completely.

Orange and Honey Tea Bread

MAKES 1 LOAF

13½ oz (385 g) plain flour

2½ teaspoons baking powder

½ teaspoon bicarbonate of soda

½ teaspoon salt

1 oz (30 g) margarine

8 fl oz (250 ml) clear honey

1 egg, at room temperature, lightly beaten

1½ tablespoons grated orange rind

6 fl oz (175 ml) freshly squeezed orange juice

4 oz (115 g) walnuts, chopped

1 Preheat a 325°F/170°C/Gas 3 oven.

2 Sift together the flour, baking powder, bicarbonate of soda and salt.

3 Line the bottom and sides of a 9 × 5 in (23 × 13 cm) loaf tin with greaseproof paper and grease.

4 ▲ With an electric mixer, cream the margarine until soft. Stir in the honey until blended, then stir in the egg. Add the orange rind and stir to combine thoroughly.

5 ▲ Fold the flour mixture into the honey and egg mixture in 3 batches, alternating with the orange juice. Stir in the walnuts.

6 Pour into the tin and bake until a skewer inserted in the centre comes out clean, 60–70 minutes. Let stand 10 minutes before turning out onto a rack to cool.

Spicy Apple Loaf

MAKES 1 LOAF

1 egg

8 fl oz (250 ml) bottled or homemade apple sauce

2 oz (55 g) butter or margarine, melted

3¾ oz (110 g) dark brown sugar

1¾ oz (50 g) caster sugar

10 oz (285 g) plain flour

2 teaspoons baking powder

½ teaspoon bicarbonate of soda

½ teaspoon salt

1 teaspoon ground cinnamon

½ teaspoon grated nutmeg

2½ oz (70 g) currants or raisins

2 oz (55 g) pecans or walnuts, chopped

1 Preheat a 350°F/180°C/Gas 4 oven. Line a 9 × 5 in (23 × 13 cm) loaf tin with greaseproof paper and grease.

2 ▲ Break the egg into a bowl and beat lightly. Stir in the apple sauce, butter or margarine and both sugars. Set aside.

3 In another bowl, sift together the flour, baking powder, bicarbonate of soda, salt, cinnamon and nutmeg. Fold dry ingredients into the apple sauce mixture in 3 batches.

4 ▼ Stir in the currants or raisins, and nuts.

5 Pour into the prepared tin and bake until a skewer inserted in the centre comes out clean, about 1 hour. Let stand 10 minutes. Turn out onto a rack and cool completely.

Glazed Banana Spice Loaf

MAKES 1 LOAF

1 large ripe banana

4 oz (115 g) butter, at room temperature

5½ oz (150 g) caster sugar

2 eggs, at room temperature

7½ oz (215 g) plain flour

1 teaspoon salt

1 teaspoon bicarbonate of soda

½ teaspoon grated nutmeg

¼ teaspoon ground allspice

¼ teaspoon ground cloves

6 fl oz (175 ml) soured cream

1 teaspoon vanilla essence

FOR THE GLAZE

4 oz (115 g) icing sugar

1–2 tablespoons lemon juice

1 Preheat a 350°F/180°C/Gas 4 oven. Line an 8½ × 4½ in (21.5 × 11.5 cm) loaf tin with greaseproof and grease.

2 ▼ With a fork, mash the banana in a bowl. Set aside.

3 With an electric mixer, cream the butter and sugar until light and fluffy. Add the eggs, 1 at a time, beating to blend well after each addition.

4 Sift together the flour, salt, bicarbonate of soda, nutmeg, allspice and cloves. Add to the butter mixture and stir to combine well.

5 ▲ Add the soured cream, banana, and vanilla and mix just enough to blend. Pour into the prepared tin.

6 ▲ Bake until the top springs back when touched lightly, 45–50 minutes. Let cool in the pan for 10 minutes. Turn out onto wire rack to cool.

7 ▲ For the glaze, combine the icing sugar and lemon juice, then stir until smooth.

8 To glaze, place the cooled loaf on a rack set over a baking sheet. Pour the glaze over the top of the loaf and allow to set.

Chocolate Chip Walnut Loaf

MAKES 1 LOAF

3½ oz (100 g) caster sugar

3½ oz (100 g) flour

1 teaspoon baking powder

4 tablespoons cornflour

4½ oz (130 g) butter, at room temperature

2 eggs, at room temperature

1 teaspoon vanilla extract

2 tablespoons currants or raisins

1 oz (30 g) walnuts, finely chopped

grated rind of ½ lemon

3 tablespoons plain chocolate chips

icing sugar, for dusting

1 Preheat the oven to 350°F/180°C/ Gas 4. Grease and line an 8½ × 4½ in (22 × 12 cm) loaf tin.

2 ▲ Sprinkle 1½ tablespoons of the caster sugar into the pan and tilt to distribute the sugar in an even layer over the bottom and sides. Shake out any excess.

3 ▼ Sift together the flour, baking powder and cornflour into a mixing bowl, 3 times. Set aside.

4 With an electric mixer, cream the butter until soft. Add the remaining sugar and continue beating until light and fluffy. Add the eggs, 1 at a time, beating to incorporate thoroughly after each addition.

5 Gently fold the dry ingredients into the butter mixture, in 3 batches; do not overmix.

6 ▲ Fold in the vanilla, currants or raisins, walnuts, lemon rind, and chocolate chips until just blended.

7 Pour the mixture into the prepared tin and bake until a cake tester inserted in the centre comes out clean, 45–50 minutes. Let cool in the tin for 5 minutes before transferring to a rack to cool completely. Dust over an even layer of icing sugar before serving.

Date and Nut Malt Loaf

MAKES 2 × 1 LB LOAVES

11 oz (300 g) strong plain flour

10 oz (285 g) strong plain wholemeal flour

1 teaspoon salt

3 oz (85 g) soft brown sugar

1 sachet easy-blend dried yeast

2 oz (55 g) butter or margarine

1 tablespoon black treacle

4 tablespoons malt extract

scant 8 fl oz (250 ml) lukewarm milk

4 oz (120 g) chopped dates

3 oz (85 g) sultanas

3 oz (85 g) raisins

2 oz (55 g) chopped nuts

2 tablespoons clear honey, to glaze

1 Sift the flours and salt into a large bowl, then tip in the wheat flakes that are caught in the sieve. Stir in the sugar and yeast.

2 ▲ Put the butter or margarine in a small pan with the treacle and malt extract. Stir over a low heat until melted. Leave to cool, then combine with the milk.

3 Stir the liquid into the dry ingredients and knead thoroughly for 15 minutes until the dough is elastic. (If you have a dough blade on your food processor, follow the manufacturer's instructions for timings.)

4 ▲ Knead in the fruits and nuts. Transfer the dough to an oiled bowl, cover with clear film and leave in a warm place for about 1½ hours, until the dough has doubled in size.

5 ▲ Grease two 1 lb (450 g) loaf tins. Knock back the dough and knead lightly. Divide in half, form into loaves and place in the tins. Cover and leave in a warm place for about 30 minutes, until risen. Meanwhile, preheat the oven to 375°F/190°C/ Gas 5.

6 Bake for 35–40 minutes, until well risen and sounding hollow when tapped underneath. Cool on a wire rack. Brush with honey while warm.

Gingerbread

SERVES 8–10

1 tablespoon vinegar
6 fl oz (175 ml) milk
7 oz (200 g) flour
2 teaspoons baking powder
¼ teaspoon bicarbonate of soda
½ teaspoon salt
2 teaspoons ground ginger
1 teaspoon ground cinnamon
¼ teaspoon ground cloves
4 oz (120 g) butter, at room temperature
3½ oz (100 g) caster sugar
1 egg, at room temperature
8 oz (225 g) molasses
whipped cream, for serving
chopped stem ginger, for decorating

1 ▲ Preheat the oven to 350°F/ 180°C/Gas 4. Line the base of an 8 in (20 cm) square cake tin with greaseproof paper and grease the paper and sides of the tin.

2 ▲ Add the vinegar to the milk and set aside. It will curdle.

3 In another mixing bowl, sift all the dry ingredients together 3 times and set aside.

4 With an electric mixer, cream the butter and sugar until light and fluffy. Beat in the egg until well combined.

5 ▼ Stir in the molasses.

6 ▲ Fold in the dry ingredients in 4 batches, alternating with the curdled milk. Mix only enough to blend.

7 Pour into the prepared tin and bake until firm, 45–50 minutes. Cut into squares and serve warm, with whipped cream. Decorate with the stem ginger.

Mango Tea Bread

MAKES 2 LOAVES

10 oz (285 g) plain flour
2 teaspoons bicarbonate of soda
2 teaspoons ground cinnamon
½ teaspoon salt
4 oz (115 g) margarine, at room temperature
3 eggs, at room temperature
10½ oz (300 g) sugar
4 fl oz (125 ml) vegetable oil
1 large ripe mango, peeled and chopped
3¼ oz (90 g) desiccated coconut
2½ oz (70 g) raisins

1 Preheat the oven to 350°F/180°C/ Gas 4. Line the bottom and sides of 2 9 × 5 in (23 × 13 cm) loaf tins with greaseproof paper and grease.

2 Sift together the flour, bicarbonate of soda, cinnamon and salt. Set aside.

3 With an electric mixer, cream the margarine until soft.

4 ▼ Beat in the eggs and sugar until light and fluffy. Beat in the oil.

5 Fold the dry ingredients into the creamed ingredients in 3 batches.

6 Fold in the mangoes, two-thirds of the coconut and the raisins.

7 ▲ Spoon the batter into the pans.

8 Sprinkle over the remaining coconut. Bake until a skewer inserted in the centre comes out clean, 50–60 minutes. Let stand for 10 minutes before turning out onto a rack to cool completely.

Courgette Tea Bread

MAKES 1 LOAF

2 oz (55 g) butter
3 eggs
8 fl oz (250 ml) vegetable oil
10½ oz (300 g) sugar
2 medium unpeeled courgettes, grated
10 oz (285 g) plain flour
2 teaspoons bicarbonate of soda
1 teaspoon baking powder
1 teaspoon salt
1 teaspoon ground cinnamon
1 teaspoon grated nutmeg
¼ teaspoon ground cloves
4 oz (115 g) walnuts, chopped

1 Preheat the oven to 350°F/180°C/ Gas 4.

2 Line the bottom and sides of a 9 × 5 in (23 × 13 cm) loaf tin with greaseproof paper and grease.

3 ▲ In a saucepan, melt the butter over low heat. Set aside.

4 With an electric mixer, beat the eggs and oil together until thick. Beat in the sugar. Stir in the melted butter and courgettes. Set aside.

5 ▲ In another bowl, sift all the dry ingredients together 3 times. Carefully fold into the courgette mixture. Fold in the walnuts.

6 Pour into the tin and bake until a skewer inserted in the centre comes out clean, 60–70 minutes. Let stand 10 minutes before turning out onto wire rack to cool completely.

Pineapple and Apricot Cake

SERVES 10–12

6 oz (170 g) unsalted butter

5 oz (150 g) caster sugar

3 eggs, beaten

few drops of vanilla essence

8 oz (225 g) plain flour, sifted

¼ teaspoon salt

1½ teaspoons baking powder

8 oz (225 g) ready-to-eat dried apricots, chopped

4 oz (120 g) each chopped crystallized ginger and crystallized pineapple

grated rind and juice of ½ orange

grated rind and juice of ½ lemon

a little milk

1 ▲ Preheat the oven to 350°F/ 180°C/Gas 4. Double line an 8 in (20 cm) round or 7 in (18 cm) square cake tin. Cream the butter and sugar together until light and fluffy.

2 Gradually beat the eggs into the creamed mixture with the vanilla essence, beating well after each addition. Sift together the flour, salt and baking powder, and add a little with the last of the egg, then fold in the rest.

3 ▲ Fold in the fruit, crystallized fruit and fruit rinds gently, then add sufficient fruit juice and milk to give a fairly soft dropping consistency.

4 ▲ Spoon into the prepared tin and smooth the top with a wet spoon. Bake for 20 minutes, then reduce the heat to 325°F/160°C/Gas 3 for a further 1½–2 hours, or until firm to the touch and a skewer comes out of the centre clean. Leave the cake to cool in the tin, turn out and wrap in fresh paper before storing in an airtight tin.

> **~ COOK'S TIP ~**
>
> This is not a long-keeping cake, but it does freeze, well-wrapped in greaseproof paper and then foil.

Banana Bread

MAKES 1 LOAF

7 oz (200 g) plain flour
2¼ teaspoons baking powder
½ teaspoon salt
¾ teaspoon ground cinnamon (optional)
4 tablespoons wheat germ
2½ oz (75 g) butter or margarine, at room temperature
4 oz (115 g) caster sugar
¾ teaspoon grated lemon zest
3 ripe bananas, mashed
2 eggs, beaten to mix

1 Preheat a 350°F/180°C/Gas 4 oven. Grease and flour an 8½ × 4½ in (21 × 11 cm) loaf tin.

2 ▲ Sift the flour, baking powder, salt and cinnamon, if using, into a bowl. Stir in the wheat germ.

3 ▲ In another bowl, combine the butter or margarine with the sugar and lemon zest. Beat until the mixture is light and fluffy.

4 ▲ Add the mashed bananas and eggs and mix well.

5 Add the dry ingredients and blend quickly and evenly.

~ **VARIATION** ~

For Banana Walnut Bread, add 2–3 oz (55–85 g) finely chopped walnuts with the dry ingredients.

6 ▼ Spoon into the prepared loaf tin. Bake for 50–60 minutes or until a wooden skewer inserted in the centre comes out clean.

7 Cool in the pan for about 5 minutes, then turn out on to a wire rack to cool completely.

Banana Orange Loaf

MAKES 1 LOAF

3½ oz (100 g) wholemeal plain flour

3½ oz (100 g) plain flour

1 teaspoon baking powder

1 teaspoon mixed spice

3 tablespoons flaked hazelnuts, toasted

2 large ripe bananas

1 egg

2 tablespoons sunflower oil

2 tablespoons clear honey

finely grated rind and juice 1 small
    orange

4 orange slices, halved

2 teaspoons icing sugar

1 ▼ Preheat the oven to 350°F/
180°C/Gas 4. Brush a 1¼ pint (750 ml)
loaf tin with sunflower oil and line the
base with non-stick baking paper.

2 ▲ Sift the flours with the baking
powder and spice into a large bowl,
adding any bran that is caught in the
sieve. Stir the hazelnuts into the
dry ingredients.

3 ▲ Peel and mash the bananas.
Beat in the egg, oil, honey and the
orange rind and juice. Stir evenly
into the dry ingredients.

4 Spoon into the prepared tin and
smooth the top. Bake for 40–45
minutes, or until firm and golden
brown. Turn out and cool on a wire
rack to cool.

5 Sprinkle the orange slices with the
icing sugar and grill until golden. Use
to decorate the cake.

~ COOK'S TIP ~

If you plan to keep the loaf for
more than two or three days, omit
the orange slices, brush with honey
and sprinkle with flaked hazelnuts.

Spiced Date and Walnut Bread

Makes 1 loaf

11 oz (300 g) wholemeal self-raising flour
2 teaspoons mixed spice
5 oz (150 g) chopped dates
2 oz (55 g) chopped walnuts
4 tablespoons sunflower oil
4 oz (120 g) dark muscovado sugar
½ pint (300 ml) skimmed milk
walnut halves, to decorate

1 Preheat the oven to 350°F/180°C/ Gas 4. Grease and line a 2 lb (900 g) loaf tin with greaseproof paper.

2 ▲ Sift together the flour and spice, adding back any bran from the sieve. Stir in the dates and walnuts.

3 ▲ Mix the oil, sugar and milk, then stir evenly into the dry ingredients.

4 ▲ Spoon into the prepared tin and arrange the walnut halves on top.

5 Bake the cake in the oven for about 45–50 minutes, or until golden brown and firm. Turn out the cake, remove the lining paper and leave to cool on a wire rack.

~ COOK'S TIP ~

Pecan nuts can be used in place of the walnuts in this bread.

Banana and Oat Gingerbread

MAKES 1 LOAF

7 oz (200 g) plain flour

2 teaspoons bicarbonate of soda

2 teaspoons ground ginger

5 oz (150 g) medium oatmeal

4 tablespoons dark muscovado sugar

3 oz (85 g) sunflower margarine

5 oz (150 g) golden syrup

1 egg, beaten

3 ripe bananas, mashed

3 oz (85 g) icing sugar

stem ginger, to decorate

1 Preheat the oven to 325°F/160°C/ Gas 3. Grease and line a 7 × 11 in (18 × 28 cm) cake tin.

2 ▼ Sift together the flour, bicarbonate of soda and ginger, then stir in the oatmeal. Melt the sugar, margarine and syrup in a saucepan, then stir into the flour mixture. Beat in the egg and mashed bananas.

3 ▲ Spoon into the tin and bake for about 1 hour, or until firm to the touch. Allow to cool in the tin, then turn out and cut into squares.

4 ▲ Sift the icing sugar into a bowl and stir in just enough water to make a smooth, runny icing. Drizzle the icing over each square and top with a piece of stem ginger, if you like.

~ **COOK'S TIP** ~

This is a nutritious, energy-giving cake that is a good choice for packed lunches as it doesn't break up too easily. This gingerbread keeps well, stored in a covered container for up to 2 months.

Dried Fruit Tea Bread

MAKES 1

6 oz (170 g) roughly chopped dried fruit salad mixture, e.g. apples, apricots, prunes and peaches

8 fl oz (250 ml) hot tea

8 oz (225 g) wholemeal self-raising flour

1 teaspoon grated nutmeg

2 oz (55 g) dark muscovado sugar

3 tablespoons sunflower oil

3 tablespoons skimmed milk

demerara sugar, to sprinkle

1 ▲ Soak the dried fruits in the tea for several hours or overnight. Drain and reserve the liquid.

2 Preheat the oven to 350°F/180°C/Gas 4. Grease a 7 in (18 cm) round cake tin and line the base with non-stick baking paper.

4 ▼ Spoon the mixture into the prepared tin and sprinkle with demerara sugar. Bake for 50–55 minutes or until firm. Turn out and cool on a wire rack.

3 ▲ Sift the flour into a bowl with the nutmeg. Stir in the muscovado sugar, fruit and tea. Add the oil and milk and mix well.

> **~ VARIATION ~**
>
> For a tropical flavour, substitute dried mango, papaya, and pineapple for the dried fruit mixture, and dark rum instead of the skimmed milk. Make in an 8-in loaf tin instead of the round cake tin.

Walnut and Whisky Loaf

MAKES 1 LOAF

6 oz (170 g) walnuts, chopped
3 oz (85 g) raisins, chopped
3 oz (85 g) currants
4 oz (120 g) flour
1 teaspoon baking powder
¼ teaspoon salt
4 oz (120 g) butter
7 oz (200 g) caster sugar
3 eggs, at room temperature, separated
1 teaspoon grated nutmeg
½ teaspoon ground cinnamon
5 tablespoons whisky
icing sugar, for dusting

1 ▼ Preheat the oven to 325°F/160°C/Gas 3. Line the base of a 9 × 5 in (23 × 13 cm) loaf tin and grease the base and sides.

2 ▲ Place the walnuts, raisins, and currants in a bowl. Sprinkle over 2 tablespoons of the flour, mix and set aside. Sift together the remaining flour, baking powder, and salt.

3 ▲ Cream the butter and sugar until light and fluffy. Beat in the egg yolks.

4 Mix the nutmeg, cinnamon, and whisky. Fold into the butter mixture, alternating with the flour mixture.

5 ▲ In another bowl, beat the egg whites until stiff. Fold into the whisky mixture until just blended. Fold in the walnut mixture.

6 Bake until a cake tester inserted in the centre comes out clean, about 1 hour. Let cool in the tin. Dust with icing sugar over a template.

Sweet Sesame Loaf

MAKES 1 OR 2 LOAVES

3 oz (85 g) sesame seeds

10 oz (285 g) plain flour

2½ teaspoons baking powder

1 teaspoon salt

2 oz (55 g) butter or margarine, at room
temperature

4½ oz (125 g) sugar

2 eggs, at room temperature

grated rind of 1 lemon

12 fl oz (350 ml) milk

1 Preheat a 350°F/180°C/Gas 4 oven.
Line a 9 × 5 in (23 × 13 cm) loaf tin
with greaseproof paper and grease.

2 ▲ Reserve 2 tablespoons of the
sesame seeds. Spread the rest on a
baking sheet and bake until lightly
toasted, about 10 minutes.

3 Sift the flour, salt and baking
powder into a bowl.

4 ▲ Stir in the toasted sesame seeds
and set aside.

5 With an electric mixer, cream the
butter or margarine and sugar together
until light and fluffy. Beat in the eggs,
then stir in the lemon rind and milk.

6 ▼ Pour the milk mixture over the
dry ingredients and fold in with a large
metal spoon until just blended.

7 ▲ Pour into the tin and sprinkle
over the reserved sesame seeds.

8 Bake until a skewer inserted in the
centre comes out clean, about 1 hour.
Let cool in the tin for 10 minutes.
Turn out onto wire rack to cool
completely.

SAVOURY
MUFFINS & BREADS

Quick and easy to make, light, fragrant muffins and
breads are ideal for packed lunches, brunches or picnics.
Use Rosemary Focaccia to make a satisfying sandwich
with an Italian flavour, and serve Tomato or
Italian Bread Sticks with soups and stews.
Try Bacon and Cornmeal Muffins – packed with
protein for a fortifying breakfast.

Cheese Muffins

MAKES 9

2 oz (55 g) butter

7 oz (200 g) plain flour

2 teaspoons baking powder

2 tablespoons sugar

¼ teaspoon salt

1 teaspoon paprika

2 eggs

4 fl oz (125 ml) milk

1 teaspoon dried thyme

2 oz (55 g) mature Cheddar cheese, cut into ½ in (1 cm) dice

1 Preheat the oven to 375°F/190°C/ Gas 5. Thickly grease 9 deep muffin tins or use paper cases.

2 Melt the butter and set aside.

3 ▼ In a mixing bowl, sift together the flour, baking powder, sugar, salt and paprika.

4 ▲ In another bowl, combine the eggs, milk, melted butter and thyme, and whisk to blend.

5 Add the milk mixture to the dry ingredients and stir just until moistened; do not mix until smooth.

6 ▲ Place a heaped spoonful of batter into the prepared cups. Drop a few pieces of cheese over each, then top with another spoonful of batter. For even baking, half-fill any empty muffin cups with water.

7 ▲ Bake until puffed and golden, about 25 minutes. Let stand 5 minutes before unmoulding on to a rack. Serve warm or at room temperature.

Bacon and Cornmeal Muffins

MAKES 14

8 bacon rashers

2 oz (55 g) butter

2 oz (55 g) margarine

4 oz (120 g) plain flour

1 tablespoon baking powder

1 teaspoon sugar

¼ teaspoon salt

8 oz (225 g) cornmeal

4 fl oz (125 ml) milk

2 eggs

1 Preheat the oven to 400°F/200°C/
Gas 6. Lightly grease 14 deep muffin
tins or use paper cases.

2 ▲ Fry the bacon until crisp. Drain
on kitchen paper, then chop into
small pieces. Set aside.

3 Gently melt the butter and
margarine and set aside.

4 ▲ Sift the flour, baking powder,
sugar, and salt into a large mixing
bowl. Stir in the cornmeal, then make
a well in the centre.

5 In a saucepan, heat the milk to
lukewarm. In a small bowl, lightly
whisk the eggs, then add to the milk.
Stir in the melted fats.

6 ▼ Pour the milk mixture into the
centre of the well and stir until
smooth and well blended.

7 ▲ Stir the bacon into the mixture,
then spoon the mixture into the
prepared cups, filling them half-full.
Bake until risen and lightly coloured,
about 20 minutes. Serve hot or warm.

Rosemary Bread

MAKES 1 LOAF

1 sachet easy-blend dried yeast

6 oz (170 g) wholemeal flour

6 oz (170 g) self-raising flour

2 tablespoons butter, plus more to grease bowl and tin

4 tablespoons warm water (110°F/45°C)

8 fl oz (250 ml) milk, at room temperature

1 tablespoon sugar

1 teaspoon salt

1 tablespoon sesame seeds

1 tablespoon dried chopped onion

1 tablespoon fresh rosemary leaves, plus more to garnish

4 oz (120 g) Cheddar cheese, cubed

coarse salt, to garnish

1 ▼ Mix the yeast with the flours in a large mixing bowl. Melt the butter. Stir in the warm water, milk, sugar, butter, salt, sesame seeds, onion and rosemary, then knead thoroughly until quite smooth.

2 ▲ Flatten the dough, then add the cheese cubes. Quickly knead them in until they have been well combined.

3 Place the dough into a clean bowl greased with a little butter, turning it so that it becomes greased on all sides. Cover with a clean, dry cloth. Put the greased bowl and dough in a warm place for about 1½ hours, or until the dough has risen and doubled in size.

4 Grease a 9 × 5 in (23 × 13 cm) loaf tin with the remaining butter. Knock down the dough to remove some of the air, and shape it into a loaf. Put the loaf into the tin, cover with a clean cloth and leave for about 1 hour until doubled in size. Preheat the oven to 375°F/190°C/Gas 5.

5 Bake for 30 minutes. During the last 5–10 minutes of baking, cover the loaf with foil to prevent it from becoming too dark. Remove the loaf from the tin and leave to cool on a wire rack. Scatter a few rosemary leaves and some coarse salt on top.

~ **VARIATION** ~

For Tarragon Bread, substitute 1 tablespoon chopped fresh tarragon for the rosemary, and 4 oz (120 g) goat's cheese for the Cheddar.

Orange Wheat Loaf

MAKES ONE 1 LB (450 G) LOAF

10 oz (285 g) wholemeal plain flour

½ teaspoon salt

1 oz (30 g) butter

2 tablespoons soft light brown sugar

½ sachet easy-blend dried yeast

grated rind and juice of ½ orange

1 ▲ Sift the flour into a large bowl and return any wheat flakes from the sieve. Add the salt and rub in the butter lightly with your fingertips.

2 ▲ Stir in the sugar, yeast and orange rind. Pour the orange juice into a measuring jug and make up to 7 fl oz (200 ml) with hot water (the liquid should not be more than hand hot). Stir the liquid into the flour and mix to a soft ball of dough.

3 ▼ Turn out the dough on to a lightly floured surface and knead until quite smooth.

4 Place the dough in a greased 1 lb (450 g) loaf tin and leave in a warm place until nearly doubled in size. Preheat the oven to 425°F/220°C/ Gas 7.

5 Bake the bread for 30–35 minutes, or until it sounds hollow when you tap the underneath. Tip out of the tin and cool on a wire rack.

~ **FREEZER NOTE** ~

To freeze, wrap tightly in foil when still warm, then leave to cool completely before freezing. Keeps for up to one year.

Corn Bread

MAKES 1 LOAF

4 oz (115 g) plain flour

2½ oz (75 g) caster sugar

1 teaspoon salt

1 tablespoon baking powder

6 oz (170 g) cornmeal, or polenta

12 fl oz (350 ml) milk

2 eggs

3 oz (85 g) butter, melted

4 oz (115 g) margarine, melted

1 Preheat a 400°F/200°C/Gas 6 oven. Line a 9 × 5 in (23 × 13 cm) loaf tin with greaseproof paper and grease.

2 Sift the flour, sugar, salt and baking powder into a mixing bowl.

3 ▼ Add the cornmeal and stir to blend. Make a well in the centre.

4 ▲ Whisk together the milk, eggs, butter and margarine. Pour the mixture into the well. Stir until just blended; do not overmix.

5 Pour into the tin and bake until a skewer inserted in the centre comes out clean, about 45 minutes. Serve hot or at room temperature.

Spicy Sweetcorn Bread

MAKES 9 SQUARES

3–4 whole canned chilli peppers, drained

2 eggs

16 fl oz (450 ml) buttermilk

2 oz (55 g) butter, melted

2 oz (55 g) plain flour

1 teaspoon bicarbonate of soda

2 teaspoons salt

6 oz (170 g) cornmeal, or polenta

12 oz (350 g) canned sweetcorn or frozen sweetcorn, thawed

1 Preheat a 400°F/200°C/Gas 6 oven. Line the bottom and sides of a 9 in (23 cm) square cake tin with greaseproof paper and grease lightly.

2 ▲ With a sharp knife, finely chop the chillies and set aside.

3 ▲ In a large bowl, whisk the eggs until frothy, then whisk in the buttermilk. Add the melted butter.

4 In another large bowl, sift together the flour, bicarbonate of soda and salt. Fold into the buttermilk mixture in 3 batches, then fold in the cornmeal in 3 batches.

5 ▲ Fold in the chillies and sweetcorn.

6 Pour the mixture into the prepared tin and bake until a skewer inserted in the middle comes out clean, 25–30 minutes. Let stand for 2–3 minutes before unmoulding. Cut into squares and serve warm.

Brown Soda Bread

M_AKES_ ONE 2 _LB_ (1 _KG_) _LOAF_

1 lb (450 g) plain flour
1 lb (450 g) wholemeal flour
2 teaspoons salt
1 tablespoon bicarbonate of soda
4 teaspoons cream of tartar
2 teaspoons caster sugar
2 oz (55 g) butter
about 1½ pints (900 ml) buttermilk or skimmed milk
extra wholemeal flour, to sprinkle

1 Lightly grease a baking sheet. Preheat the oven to 375°F/190°C/ Gas 5.

2 ▼ Sift all the dry ingredients into a large bowl, tipping any bran from the flour back into the bowl.

3 ▲ Rub the butter into the flour mixture, then add enough buttermilk or milk to make a soft dough. You may not need all of it, so add it cautiously.

4 ▲ Knead lightly until smooth then transfer to the baking sheet and shape to a large round about 2 in (5 cm) thick.

5 ▲ Using the floured handle of a wooden spoon, form a large cross on top of the dough. Sprinkle over a little extra wholemeal flour.

6 Bake for 40–50 minutes until risen and firm. Cool for 5 minutes before transferring to a wire rack to cool further.

Sage Soda Bread

MAKES 1 LOAF

8 oz (225 g) wholemeal flour

4 oz (120 g) strong white flour

½ teaspoon salt

1 teaspoon bicarbonate of soda

2 tablespoons shredded fresh sage

½–¾ pint (300–450 ml) buttermilk

3 ▼ Shape the dough into a round loaf and place on a lightly oiled baking sheet.

4 ▲ Cut a deep cross in the top. Bake in the oven for 40 minutes until the loaf is well risen and sounds hollow when tapped on the bottom. Leave to cool on a wire rack.

1 ▲ Preheat the oven to 425°F/220°C/Gas 7. Sift the dry ingredients into a bowl.

2 ▲ Stir in the sage and add enough of the buttermilk to make a soft dough.

~ **COOK'S TIP** ~

As an alternative to the sage, try using finely chopped fresh rosemary or thyme.

Courgette Crown Bread

SERVES 8

1 lb (450 g) courgettes, coarsely grated

salt

1¼ lb (500 g) plain flour

2 sachets easy-blend dried yeast

4 tablespoons freshly grated Parmesan cheese

2 tablespoons olive oil

black pepper

milk, to glaze

sesame seeds, to garnish

1 Layer the courgettes in a colander and sprinkle them lightly with salt. Leave to drain for 30 minutes, then pat dry.

2 Grease and line a 9 in (23 cm) round sandwich tin. Preheat the oven to 400°F/200°C/Gas 6. In a large mixing bowl, mix the flour, yeast and Parmesan cheese together and season with black pepper.

3 ▲ Stir in the oil and courgettes and add enough lukewarm water to give a firm dough. Knead on a floured surface until smooth.

4 ▲ Leave it to rise in a warm place until doubled in size. Break into eight balls, rolling each one and placing them in the tin as shown. Brush the tops with milk and sprinkle over the sesame seeds.

5 Allow to rise again, then bake the bread for 25 minutes or until golden brown. Cool slightly in the tin, then turn out the bread to cool further.

Rosemary Focaccia

SERVES 4

1 lb (450 g) packet white bread mix

4 tablespoons extra virgin olive oil

2 teaspoons dried rosemary, crushed

8 sun-dried tomatoes, snipped

12 black olives, stoned and chopped

7 fl oz (200 ml) lukewarm water

sea salt flakes

~ **VARIATION** ~

For Gremolata Focaccia, substitute 2 tablespoons chopped fresh parsley for the rosemary, 2 tablespoons capers for the sun-dried tomatoes, and add 1 crushed garlic clove to the dough.

1 ▲ Mix the bread mix with half the oil, the rosemary, tomatoes, olives and water until it forms a firm dough.

2 Turn out the dough on to a floured surface and knead for 5 minutes. Return to the mixing bowl and cover with oiled clear film.

3 Leave the dough to rise in a warm place until it has doubled in size. Meanwhile, lightly grease two baking sheets and preheat the oven to 425°F/220°C/Gas 7.

4 ▼ Turn out the risen dough, punch down and knead again. Divide into two and shape into rounds. Place on the baking sheet, and punch hollows in the dough. Trickle over the remaining olive oil and sprinkle with salt.

5 Bake the focaccia for 12–15 minutes until golden brown and cooked. Slide off on to wire racks to cool. Eat slightly warm.

Focaccia with Onions

SERVES 6–8

1 lb (450 g) plain flour

1 sachet easy-blend dried yeast

1 teaspoon salt

pinch of sugar

5 tablespoons olive oil

1 medium onion, sliced very thinly and cut into short lengths

½ teaspoon fresh thyme leaves

coarse sea salt

1 Place the flour, yeast, salt and sugar in a bowl. Make a well in the centre and pour in 8 fl oz (250 ml) lukewarm water and 1 tablespoon of the oil. Mix to a dough and knead on a floured surface until smooth and elastic.

2 Place the dough in a large oiled bowl, cover with clear film and leave in a warm place until doubled in size. Turn out the dough on to a floured surface and knead for 3–4 minutes.

3 ▼ After punching the dough down, knead it for 3–4 minutes. Brush a large shallow baking pan with 1 tablespoon of the oil. Place the dough in the pan, and use your fingers to press it into an even layer 1 in (2 cm) thick. Cover the dough with a cloth, and leave to rise in a warm place for 30 minutes. Preheat the oven to 400°F/200°C/Gas 6 during this time.

4 ▲ While the focaccia is rising, heat 3 tablespoons of the oil in a medium frying pan. Add the onion, and cook over low heat until soft. Stir in the thyme.

5 ▲ Just before baking, use your fingers to press rows of light indentations into the surface of the focaccia. Brush with the remaining oil.

6 ▲ Spread the onions evenly over the top, and sprinkle lightly with coarse salt. Bake for about 25 minutes, or until just golden. Cut into squares or wedges and serve as an accompaniment to a meal, or alone, warm or at room temperature.

Courgette and Parmesan Bread

MAKES 1 LOAF

5 oz (150 g) plain flour
5 oz (150 g) wholemeal flour
2 teaspoons baking powder
1 teaspoon salt
1 teaspoon ground cumin
1 teaspoon fennel seeds
2 medium courgettes, about 8 oz (225 g), grated
¼ pint (150 ml) vegetable oil
2 eggs, beaten
3 tablespoons milk
2 oz (55 g) grated Parmesan cheese
1 teaspoon sesame seeds
salt and black pepper

1 ▲ Preheat the oven to 350°F/ 180°C/Gas 4. Grease a 2 lb (900 g) loaf tin and line the base. Sift the flours, baking powder, salt and cumin into a bowl and tip in any bran left in the sieve.

2 ▲ Add the fennel seeds, followed by the grated courgette.

3 ▼ Whisk together the oil, eggs, milk and half the cheese in a bowl. Stir into the courgette mixture.

4 ▲ Spoon the mixture into the prepared tin and level the top. Sprinkle the top with the remaining Parmesan cheese. Bake for 40–45 minutes, until risen and when a skewer pierced through the centre comes out clean. Serve hot or cold.

Italian Bread Sticks

MAKES ABOUT 30

½ teaspoon dried yeast
4 fl oz (125 ml) lukewarm water
pinch sugar
2 teaspoons malt extract (optional)
1 teaspoon salt
7–8 oz (200–225 g) plain flour

1 ▲ Warm a medium mixing bowl by swirling some hot water in it. Drain. Place the yeast in the bowl, and pour on the warm water. Stir in the sugar, mix with a fork, and allow to stand until the yeast has dissolved and starts to foam, 5–10 minutes.

2 ▲ Use a wooden spoon to mix in the malt extract, if using, the salt and about one-third of the flour. Mix in another third of the flour, stirring with the spoon until the dough forms a mass and begins to pull away from the sides of the bowl.

3 ▲ Sprinkle some of the remaining flour onto a smooth work surface. Remove all of the dough from the bowl, and begin to knead it, working in the remaining flour a little at a time. Knead for 8–10 minutes. By the end the dough should be elastic and smooth. Form it into a ball.

4 ▲ Tear a lump the size of a small walnut from the ball of dough. Roll it lightly between your hands into a small sausage shape. Set it aside on a lightly floured surface. Repeat until all the dough is used up. There should be about 30 pieces.

~ **VARIATION** ~

These bread sticks are also good when rolled lightly in poppy or sesame seeds before being baked.

5 ▲ Place one piece of dough on a clean smooth work surface without any flour on it. Roll the dough under the spread-out fingers of both hands, moving your hands backwards and forwards to lengthen and thin the dough into a long strand about ½ in (1 cm) thick. Transfer to a very lightly greased baking tray. Repeat with the remaining dough pieces, taking care to roll all the sticks to about the same thickness.

6 ▲ Preheat the oven to 400°F/ 200°C/Gas 6. Cover the tray with a cloth, and place the bread sticks in a warm place to rise for 10–15 minutes while the oven is heating. Bake for about 8–10 minutes. Remove from the oven. Turn the sticks over, and return them to the oven for 6–7 minutes more. Do not let them brown. Allow to cool. Bread sticks should be crisp when served. If they lose their crispness on a damp day, warm them in a moderate oven for a few minutes before serving.

Saffron Focaccia

MAKES 1 LOAF

pinch of saffron threads
¼ pint (150 ml) boiling water
8 oz (225 g) plain flour
½ teaspoon salt
1 teaspoon easy-blend dried yeast
1 tablespoon olive oil
FOR THE TOPPING
2 garlic cloves, sliced
1 red onion, cut into thin wedges
a few rosemary sprigs
12 black olives, stoned and coarsely chopped
1 tablespoon olive oil

1 ▲ Place the saffron in a heatproof jug and pour on the boiling water. Leave to stand and infuse until lukewarm.

2 ▲ Place the flour, salt, yeast and olive oil in a food processor. Turn on and gradually add the saffron and its liquid. Process until the dough forms into a ball.

3 ▲ Turn onto a floured board and knead for 10–15 minutes. Place in a bowl, cover and leave to rise for 30–40 minutes until doubled in size.

4 ▲ Punch down the risen dough on a lightly floured surface and roll out into an oval shape, ½ in (1 cm) thick. Place on a greased baking tray and leave to rise for 20–30 minutes.

5 ▲ Preheat the oven to 400°F/200°C/Gas 6. Use your fingers to press small indentations all over the surface of the foccacia.

6 ▲ Cover with the topping ingredients, brush lightly with olive oil, and bake for 25 minutes or until the loaf sounds hollow when tapped on the bottom. Leave to cool on a wire rack.

~ VARIATION ~

For Herb Focaccia, substitute 2 tablespoons chopped fresh mixed herbs, such as parsley, thyme, chives and basil, for the rosemary. Use 2 tablespoons sun-dried tomato paste instead of the olives.

~ COOK'S TIP ~

If you only have active dried yeast in your store cupboard, place it in a bowl, then add the saffron liquid once it has cooled down to warm. Add a pinch of sugar, stir, and leave to stand until the yeast has dissolved and starts to foam. Add the flour, salt and oil, transfer mixture to a food processor and proceed as directed.

Focaccia with Olives

SERVES 6–8

FOR THE BASIC DOUGH

1 lb (450 g) plain flour

1 sachet easy-blend dried yeast

1 teaspoon salt

pinch of sugar

3 tablespoons olive oil

FOR THE TOPPING

10–12 large green olives, stoned and halved lengthways

coarse sea salt

1 Place the flour, yeast, salt and sugar in a bowl. Make a well in the centre and pour in 8 fl oz (250 ml) lukewarm water and 1 tablespoon of the oil. Mix to a dough and knead on a floured surface until smooth and elastic.

2 Place dough in a large oiled bowl, cover with clear film and leave in a warm place until doubled in size. Turn out the dough on to a floured surface and knead for 3–4 minutes.

3 Brush a large shallow baking tin with 1 tablespoon of the oil. Place the dough in the pan, and use your fingers to press it into an even layer 1 in (2 cm) thick.

4 ▲ Cover the dough with a cloth, and leave to rise in a warm place for 30 minutes. Preheat the oven to 400°F/200°C/Gas 6. Just before baking, use your fingers to press rows of light indentations into the surface of the focaccia. Brush with the remaining oil.

5 ▲ Dot evenly with the olive pieces, and sprinkle with a little coarse salt. Bake for about 25 minutes, or until just golden. Cut into squares or wedges and serve as an accompaniment to a meal, or alone, warm or at room temperature.

~ **COOK'S TIP** ~

For a delicious sandwich, split the focaccia in half, horizontally, and fill with sliced mozzarella cheese, sliced tomatoes and fresh basil leaves.

Focaccia with Rosemary

SERVES 6–8

1 quantity Basic Dough, risen once (see above)

3 tablespoons olive oil

2 sprigs fresh rosemary, coarse stalks removed

coarse sea salt

1 After punching the dough down, knead it for 3–4 minutes. Brush a large shallow baking pan with 1 tablespoon of the oil. Place the dough in the pan, and use your fingers to press it into an even layer 1 in (2 cm) thick.

2 ▲ Scatter with the rosemary leaves. Cover the dough with a cloth, and leave to rise in a warm place for 30 minutes. Preheat the oven to 400°F/200°C/Gas 6 during this time.

3 ▼ Just before baking, use your fingers to press rows of light indentations into the surface of the focaccia. Brush with the remaining oil, and sprinkle lightly with coarse salt. Bake for about 25 minutes, or until just golden. Cut into squares or wedges and serve as an accompaniment to a meal, or alone, warm or at room temperature.

Italian Olive Bread

MAKES 1 LOAF

12 oz (340 g) strong plain flour
½ teaspoon salt
1 teaspoon easy-blend dried yeast
1 teaspoon dried thyme
3 tablespoons olive oil
4 black olives, stoned and chopped
3 sun-dried tomatoes in oil, chopped
crushed rock salt

1 ▲ Place the flour and salt in a bowl and sprinkle over the yeast and thyme. Make a well in the centre and pour in 7 fl oz (200 ml) of warm water and 2 tablespoons of the olive oil.

2 Mix to a dough and knead on a floured surface for 10 minutes, until elastic (or use a food processor or a mixer with a dough attachment).

3 Place the dough in a large oiled polythene bag. Seal and leave in a warm place for about 2 hours, or until the dough has doubled in size.

4 ▲ Turn out the dough on a floured surface and knead lightly. Flatten with your hands. Sprinkle over the olives and tomatoes and knead in until well distributed. Shape the dough into a long oval and place on a greased baking sheet. Cover and leave to rise in a warm place for 45 minutes. Preheat the oven to 375°F/190°C/Gas 5.

5 ▲ When risen, press your finger several times into the dough, drizzle over the remaining oil and sprinkle with the salt. Bake for 35–40 minutes, until the loaf is golden and sounds hollow when tapped on the bottom.

Tomato Bread Sticks

Makes 16

8 oz (225 g) plain flour

½ teaspoon salt

½ tablespoon easy-blend dried yeast

1 teaspoon honey

1 teaspoon olive oil

¼ pint (150 ml) warm water

6 pieces sun-dried tomatoes in olive oil, drained and chopped

1 tablespoon skimmed milk

2 teaspoons poppy seeds

1 Place the flour, salt and yeast in a food processor. Add the honey and olive oil and, with the machine running, gradually pour in the water (you may not need it all as flours vary). Stop adding water as soon as the dough starts to cling together. Process for 1 minute more.

2 ▲ Turn out the dough on to a floured board and knead for 3–4 minutes until springy and smooth.

3 ▲ Knead in the chopped sun-dried tomatoes. Form into a ball and place in a lightly oiled bowl. Leave to rise for 30 minutes.

4 ▼ Preheat the oven to 300°F/ 150°C/Gas 2. Divide the dough into 16 pieces and roll each piece into an 11 × ½ in (28 × 1 cm) long stick. Place on a lightly oiled baking sheet and leave to rise in a warm place for 15 minutes.

5 ▲ Brush the sticks with milk and sprinkle with poppy seeds. Bake for 30 minutes. Leave to cool on a wire rack.

SCONES
& POPOVERS

At their best when warm from the oven, scones
needn't be confined to simple buttermilk or
traditional varieties. Cheese Scones, enlivened by the
addition of fresh or dried herbs, or Sunflower Sultana
Scones are some of the imaginative recipes included
here. As a change from individual Yorkshire puddings,
try tangy Parmesan Popovers for a cheesy treat.
Eat with a roast or simply as a tasty snack.

Buttermilk Scones

MAKES 15

7 oz (200 g) plain flour
1 teaspoon salt
1 teaspoon baking powder
½ teaspoon bicarbonate of soda
4 tablespoons cold butter or margarine
6 fl oz (175 ml) buttermilk

1 Preheat the oven to 425°F/220°C/ Gas 7. Grease a baking sheet.

2 Sift the dry ingredients into a bowl. Rub in the butter or margarine with your fingertips until the mixture resembles breadcrumbs.

3 ▼ Gradually pour in the buttermilk, stirring with a fork to form a soft dough.

4 ▲ Roll out the dough until about ½ in (1 cm) thick. Stamp out rounds with a 2-inch (5 cm) biscuit cutter.

5 Place on the prepared baking sheet and bake until golden, 12–15 minutes. Serve warm or at room temperature.

Traditional Sweet Scones

MAKES 8

6 oz (170 g) flour
2 tablespoons sugar
3 teaspoons baking powder
⅛ teaspoon salt
5 tablespoons cold butter, cut in pieces
4 fl oz (125 ml) milk

1 Preheat the oven to 425°F/220°C/ Gas 7. Grease a baking sheet.

2 ▲ Sift the flour, sugar, baking powder, and salt into a bowl.

3 Cut in the butter with a pastry blender until the mixture resembles coarse crumbs.

4 Pour in the milk and stir with a fork to form a soft dough.

5 ▲ Roll out the dough about ¼ in (½ cm) thick. Stamp out rounds using a 2½ in (6 cm) biscuit cutter.

6 Place on the prepared sheet and bake until golden, about 12 minutes. Serve hot or warm, with butter and jam, to accompany tea or coffee.

~ **VARIATION** ~

To make a delicious and speedy dessert, split the scones in half while still warm. Butter one half, top with lightly sugared fresh strawberries, raspberries or blueberries, and sandwich with the other half. Serve at once with dollops of whipped cream.

Cheese and Marjoram Scones

MAKES 18

4 oz (120 g) wholemeal flour

4 oz (120 g) self-raising flour

pinch of salt

1½ oz (45 g) butter

¼ teaspoon dry mustard

2 teaspoons dried marjoram

2–3 oz (55–85 g) Cheddar cheese, finely grated

4 fl oz (125 ml) milk, or as required

1 teaspoon sunflower oil

2 oz (50 g) pecan or walnuts, chopped

1 ▼ Sift the two kinds of flour into a bowl and add the salt. Cut the butter into small pieces, and rub into the flour until the mixture resembles fine breadcrumbs.

2 ▲ Add the mustard, marjoram and grated cheese, and mix in sufficient milk to make a soft dough. Knead the dough lightly.

3 Preheat the oven to 425°F/220°C/ Gas 7. Roll out the dough on a floured surface to about a ¾ in (2 cm) thickness and cut out about 18 scones using a 2 in (5 cm) square cutter. Grease two baking sheets with a little sunflower oil, and place the scones on the trays.

4 Brush the scones with a little milk and sprinkle the chopped pecans or walnuts over the top. Bake for 12 minutes. Serve warm.

~ **VARIATION** ~

For Mixed Herb and Mustard Scones, use 2 tablespoons chopped fresh parsley or chives instead of the dried marjoram and 1 teaspoon Dijon mustard instead of the dry mustard. Substitute 2 oz (50 g) chopped pistachio nuts for the pecans or walnuts.

Cheese and Chive Scones

MAKES 9

4 oz (120 g) self-raising flour

5 oz (150 g) self-raising wholemeal flour

½ teaspoon salt

3 oz (85 g) feta cheese

1 tablespoon snipped fresh chives

¼ pint (150 ml) skimmed milk, plus extra for glazing

¼ teaspoon cayenne pepper

1 ▲ Pre-heat the oven to 400°F/ 200°C/Gas 6. Sift the flours and salt into a mixing bowl, adding any bran left over from the flour in the sieve.

2 ▲ Crumble the feta cheese and rub into the dry ingredients. Stir in the chives, then add the milk and mix to a soft dough.

3 ▼ Turn out the dough on to a floured surface and lightly knead until smooth. Roll out to ¾ in (2 cm) thick and stamp out nine scones with a 2½ in (6 cm) biscuit cutter.

4 ▲ Transfer the scones to a non-stick baking sheet. Brush with skimmed milk, then sprinkle over the cayenne pepper. Bake in the oven for 15 minutes, or until golden brown. Serve warm or cold.

Wholemeal Scones

MAKES 16

6 oz (170 g) cold butter
12 oz (350 g) wholemeal flour
5 oz (140 g) plain flour
2 tablespoons sugar
½ teaspoon salt
2½ teaspoons bicarbonate of soda
2 eggs
6 fl oz (175 ml) buttermilk
1¼ oz (35 g) raisins

1 Preheat the oven to 400°F/200°C/ Gas 6. Grease and flour a large baking sheet.

2 ▲ Cut the butter into small pieces.

3 Combine the dry ingredients in a bowl. Add the butter and rub in with your fingertips until the mixture resembles coarse breadcrumbs. Set aside.

4 In another bowl, whisk together the eggs and buttermilk. Set aside 2 tablespoons for glazing.

5 Stir the remaining egg mixture into the dry ingredients until it just holds together. Stir in the raisins.

6 Roll out the dough about ¾ in (2 cm) thick. Stamp out circles with a biscuit cutter. Place on the prepared sheet and brush with the glaze.

7 Bake until golden, 12–15 minutes. Allow to cool slightly before serving. Split in two with a fork while still warm and spread with butter and jam, if wished.

Orange and Raisin Scones

MAKES 16

10 oz (285 g) plain flour
1½ tablespoons baking powder
2¼ oz (60 g) sugar
½ teaspoon salt
2½ g (70 g) butter, diced
2½ g (70 g) margarine, diced
grated rind of 1 large orange
2 oz (55 g) raisins
4 fl oz (125 ml) buttermilk
milk, for glazing

1 Preheat the oven to 425°F/220°C/ Gas 7. Grease and flour a large baking sheet.

2 Combine the dry ingredients in a large bowl. Add the butter and margarine and rub in with your fingertips until the mixture resembles coarse breadcrumbs.

3 ▲ Add the orange rind and raisins.

4 Gradually stir in the buttermilk to form a soft dough.

5 ▲ Roll out the dough about ¾ in (2 cm) thick. Stamp out circles with a biscuit cutter.

6 ▲ Place on the prepared sheet and brush the tops with milk.

7 Bake until golden, 12–15 minutes. Serve hot or warm, with butter, or whipped or clotted cream, and jam.

> **~ COOK'S TIP ~**
>
> For light tender scones, handle the dough as little as possible. If you wish, split the scones when cool and toast them under a preheated grill. Butter them while still hot.

Sunflower Sultana Scones

MAKES 10–12

8 oz (225 g) self-raising flour
1 teaspoon baking powder
1 oz (30 g) soft sunflower margarine
2 tablespoons caster sugar
2 oz (55 g) sultanas
2 tablespoons sunflower seeds
5 oz (150 g) natural yogurt
about 2–3 tablespoons skimmed milk

1 Preheat the oven to 450°F/230°C/ Gas 8. Lightly oil a baking sheet. Sift the flour and baking powder into a bowl and rub in the margarine evenly.

2 Stir in the sugar, sultanas and half the sunflower seeds, then mix in the yogurt, with just enough milk to make a fairly soft, but not sticky dough.

3 ▼ Roll out on a lightly floured surface to about ¾ in (2 cm) thickness. Cut into 2½ in (6 cm) flower shapes or rounds with a biscuit cutter and lift on to the baking sheet.

4 ▲ Brush with milk and sprinkle with the reserved sunflower seeds, then bake for 10–12 minutes, until well risen and golden brown.

5 Cool the scones on a wire rack. Serve split and spread with butter and jam.

Prune and Peel Rock Buns

MAKES 12

8 oz (225 g) plain flour
2 teaspoons baking powder
3 oz (85 g) demerara sugar
2 oz (55 g) chopped ready-to-eat dried prunes
2 oz (55 g) chopped mixed peel
finely grated rind of 1 lemon
2 fl oz (50 ml) sunflower oil
5 tablespoons skimmed milk

~ **VARIATION** ~

For Spicy Rock Buns, substitute 2 oz (50 g) currants for the ready-to-eat dried prunes, 2 oz (50 g) raisins for the mixed peel, and add 1 teaspoon mixed spice, ¼ teaspoon ground ginger, and ¼ teaspoon ground cinnamon.

1 ▼ Preheat the oven to 400°F/ 200°C/Gas 6. Lightly oil a large baking sheet. Sift together the flour and baking powder, then stir in the sugar, prunes, peel and lemon rind.

2 Mix the oil and milk, then stir into the mixture, to make a dough which just binds together.

3 ▲ Spoon into rocky heaps on the baking sheet and bake for 20 minutes, until golden. Cool on a wire rack.

Dill and Potato Cakes

MAKES 10

8 oz (225 g) self-raising flour

3 tablespoons butter, softened

pinch of salt

1 tablespoon finely chopped fresh dill

6 oz (170 g) mashed potato, freshly made

2–3 tablespoons milk, as required

1 ▼ Preheat the oven to 450°F/ 230°C/Gas 8. Sift the flour into a bowl, and add the butter, salt and dill. Mix in the mashed potato and enough milk to make a soft, pliable dough.

2 ▲ Roll out the dough on a well-floured surface until it is fairly thin. Cut into neat rounds using a 3 in (7.5 cm) cutter.

3 ▲ Grease a baking sheet, place the cakes on it, and bake for 20–25 minutes until risen and golden.

~ **VARIATION** ~

For Cheese and Herb Potato Cakes, stir in about 2 oz (55 g) crumbled blue cheese, and substitute 1 tablespoon snipped fresh chives for the dill. Mix in 3 tablespoons soured cream instead of the butter.

Parmesan Popovers

MAKES 6

2 oz (55 g) freshly grated Parmesan cheese
4 oz (120 g) plain flour
¼ teaspoon salt
2 eggs
4 fl oz (125 ml) milk
1 tablespoon melted butter or margarine

1 ▼ Preheat the oven to 450°F/
230°C/Gas 8. Grease six deep bun or
tartlet tins. Sprinkle each tin with
1 tablespoon of the grated Parmesan.
Alternatively, you can use ramekins,
heat them on a baking sheet in the
oven, then grease and sprinkle with
Parmesan just before filling.

2 Sift the flour and salt into a small
bowl. Set aside.

3 ▲ In a mixing bowl, beat together
the eggs, milk, and butter or
margarine. Add the flour mixture and
stir until smoothly blended.

4 ▼ Divide the mixture evenly
among the tins, filling each one about
half full. Bake for 15 minutes, then
sprinkle the tops of the popovers with
the remaining grated Parmesan
cheese. Reduce the heat to 350°F/
180°C/Gas 4 and continue baking
until the popovers are firm and golden
brown, 20–25 minutes.

5 ▲ Remove the popovers from the
oven. To unmould, run a thin knife
around the inside of each tin to loosen
the popovers. Gently ease out, then
transfer to a wire rack to cool.

Herb Popovers

MAKES 12

3 eggs

8 fl oz (250 ml) milk

1 oz (30 g) butter, melted

3 oz (85 g) plain flour

⅛ teaspoon salt

1 small sprig each mixed fresh herbs, such as chives, tarragon, dill and parsley

1 Preheat a 425°F/220°C/Gas 7 oven. Grease 12 small ramekins or individual baking cups.

2 With an electric mixer, beat the eggs until blended. Beat in the milk and melted butter.

3 Sift together the flour and salt, then beat into the egg mixture to combine thoroughly.

4 ▼ Strip the herb leaves from the stems and chop finely. Mix together and measure out 2 tablespoons. Stir the herbs into the batter.

5 ▲ Fill the prepared cups half-full.

6 Bake until golden, 25–30 minutes. Do not open the oven door during baking time or the popovers may collapse. For drier popovers, pierce each one with a knife after the 30 minute baking time and bake for 5 minutes more. Serve hot.

Cheese Popovers

MAKES 12

3 eggs

8 fl oz (250 ml) milk

1 oz (30 g) butter, melted

3 oz (85 g) plain flour

¼ teaspoon salt

¼ teaspoon paprika

1 oz (30 g) freshly grated Parmesan cheese

~ **VARIATION** ~

For traditional Yorkshire Pudding, omit the cheese and paprika, and use 4–6 tablespoons of beef dripping to replace the butter. Put them into the oven in time to serve warm as an accompaniment for roast beef.

1 Preheat a 425°F/220°C/Gas 7 oven. Grease 12 small ramekins.

2 ▲ With an electric mixer, beat the eggs until blended. Beat in the milk and melted butter.

3 ▲ Sift together the flour, salt and paprika, then beat into the egg mixture. Add the cheese and stir.

4 Fill the prepared cups half-full and bake until golden, 25–30 minutes. Do not open the oven door or the popovers may collapse. For drier popovers, pierce each one with a knife after the 30 minute baking time and bake for 5 minutes more. Serve hot.

INDEX

~